CREATIVE
COUNTERPART

CREATIVE COUNTERPART

Linda Dillow

Thomas Nelson Publishers
Nashville

Published in Nashville, Tennessee, by Thomas Nelson, Inc., Publishers and distributed in Canada by Lawson Falle, Ltd., Cambridge, Ontario.

Printed in the United States of America.

Thirteenth printing.

Library of Congress Cataloging in Publication Data

Dillow, Linda.
   Creative counterpart.

   Includes bibliographical references.
   1. Wives—Religious life. 2. Wives—Conduct of life. I.Title.
BV4527.D54   248'.943   76-30387
ISBN 0-8407-5617-8

Creative Counterpart Bible Study and Project Guide is available for use with this book.

   Bible verses marked KJV are taken from the King James Version.
   Verses marked NASB are from the New American Standard Bible, © The Lockman Foundation 1960, 1962, 1963, 1968, 1971, 1972, 1973, 1975, and are used by permission.
   Verses marked NIV are from the New International Version, New Testament, copyright © 1973 by the New York Bible Society International. Used by permission.
   Verses marked RSV are from the Revised Standard Version of the Bible, copyright 1946, 1952, © 1971, 1973.
   Verses marked TAB are from the Amplified New Testament, © The Lockman Foundation 1954, 1958, and are used by permission.
   Verses marked TLB are taken from the Living Bible (Wheaton, Illinois: Tyndale House Publishers, 1971) and are used by permission.

TO JODY,

MY BELOVED AND MY FRIEND,

WHOSE LOVE, ENCOURAGEMENT, AND LOGICAL MIND

MADE THIS BOOK POSSIBLE.

ACKNOWLEDGEMENTS

Many thanks to . . .

 . . . Kris Baker for her help in editing the first three chapters
 . . . Pat Acheson for her help in editing the book
 . . . Betty McFarlane for her excellent typing

Linda Dillow

CONTENTS

Jody was one of those fortunate men
who upon marrying received not only
a friend, lover, companion, and partner,
but also a "personal Holy Spirit."
This angelic being is a loving wife
who feels it is her God-ordained
responsibility to convict her husband
of sin, judgment, and righteousness
as well as instructing him in proper
etiquette, dress, and attitudes.

A Creative Counterpart reverences
her husband; a personal Holy Spirit
revamps him! This is the story of
how slowly (and many times painfully)
I learned that God gave wives
to husbands to make them happy,
and that He will make them holy!

FOREWORD

More than a decade has expired since the first salvos were fired in the renewed crusade for women's rights. We have been jarred from our complacency (and that's good!) by spasms of ink-slinging feminists picking up their standards and marching in both directions. Like reincarnated phantoms of the French Revolution, shock troops waved the banner of *Liberté, Egalité, Fraternité.* Counter crusaders responded with a simplistic white flag on which was scrawled a single word: *Submission!*

Controversy continues, and Christian wives strain to focus in on the hearings. Should we be aligned with one side or the other? Do we fight what we find, or do we surrender to it? On what basis do we decide? Futhermore, what long-term guarantee is there against depreciation?

Many of our answers are at once profound and pitifully naive. We keep asking, "What does the Bible say?" When we find out what it says, we complain that it does not fit. So we try to form it to fit our preconceived notions. Using either high-handed "scholarship" which twists the text to say what we want it to say, or a clumsy simplification which washes out to *reductio ad absurdum,* we run about mouthing fragments of "the gospel according to women."

Creative Counterpart is not a complete manual on womanhood, nor is it an exhaustive study of Christian marriage. It is a choice morsel, laced with practical fibre, for women who want to be wives in the simple manner of which the Scriptures speak, culture notwithstanding.

It has been my privilege to know Linda Dillow not only as a seminary student's wife, but as a friend and a sister in the faith of our Lord Jesus Christ. I have observed her at home as well as on the public platform. She instills confidence in the observer. With a quiet strength that exudes the fragrance of the First Peter example of womanhood, she combines inner quiet beauty with an incredible toughness of conviction. Her refined style at the rostrum reflects her inner core of cheerful dedication and good-humored discipline.

Linda does not preach. She writes neither technically nor sarcastically, but her words are an intelligent and human application of what the Bible says to wives. Her portrait of marriage is drawn with well-defined strokes which lift the role of wifehood to a level of dignity and significance.

The book has been born late in the line of apologetics for Christian marriages. Perhaps this timing allows both reader and writer an extra measure of relativity. At any rate, the one who ponders these pages will be refreshed with a cool breeze, a delightfully readable and altogether profitable discussion of marriage and homemaking.

Jeanne W. Hendricks
Dallas, Texas

CREATIVE
COUNTERPART

THE HONEYMOON DISASTER

Chapter One

The giant logging truck barreled toward us as we headed our heavily laden car up the winding road. Pulling sharply to the right, Jody missed the truck, but in the process our car landed in a ditch.

As I tried to regain composure, the events of the past three days raced through my mind: the wedding and two glorious days in the cabin on the river. Such a rustic, yet romantic place—huge fireplace, a balcony overhanging the rushing river, and, best of all, being alone with my new husband.

I could have been content to stay forever at the Hawthorne Farms cottage on the river, but such luxuries were impossible for two newly married college students. Two nights was all our budget of $200 a month would allow. Thus, to prolong our honeymoon we had decided to camp.

Mistake number one! Neither Jody nor I knew anything about camping, yet here we were, with a tent, sleeping bags, and supplies, sitting in a ditch! With Jody pushing and me steering we finally left the ditch. On the road again, we found a lovely, secluded campsite and struggled with the tent. Was this supposed to be fun?

Exhausted, we fell into our sleeping bags early, only to be awakened at midnight by a gentle rain which soon became a torrential downpour. Being *bright* college students, we soon discovered our borrowed tent had a huge leak, and we were fast on our way to being soaked! Such a delightful way to spend the third night of your honeymoon—breaking camp and packing a sopping wet tent in a downpour at 1:00 A.M.!

Romance at its height! But our problems had just begun. . . .

Driving down the mountain in the wee hours of the morning, we had a flat tire! I held the flashlight and umbrella while Jody changed the tire alongside the narrow road. He looked up at me, smiling, "Honey, I guess these are the kinds of things that bind you together in marriage!"

I look back now, thirteen years and three children later, and realize that neither Jody nor I had any idea of the many joys, sorrows, and ridiculous circumstances that would bind us as one. I had no idea of all I had to learn about loving my husband! Nor was I aware of all the "nagging" abilities that lay dormant within me!

I married Jody because I wanted to be his friend, lover, and companion forever. I've never met a woman who married because she felt it would make her miserable! Each foresees fulfillment and satisfaction with her partner. As the years pass, however, something happens. Prince Charming sometimes begins to turn into a toad or Cinderella turns into a nag, and the exciting relationship can become a daily drag.

Most women I talk with who are dissatisfied with their marriages usually point to three reasons. Number one: her husband. "If he were just more affectionate, or more aggressive, or more helpful, or more *anything,* I could be the kind of wife I should be." Number two: her circumstances. "If I lived in a bigger house, or if I *didn't* have such a big house to clean; if I had a child, or if I *didn't* have so many children," and, of course, "If we had more money, I could be a better wife." Reason number three: herself. "If I were just different —beautiful, thin, talented, successful, intelligent, creative, sexy, then I could be the wife of the year."

"But I'm me, and the daily drag will continue." That's where we're wrong! As you read these pages you will discover creative suggestions to motivate your husband, counsel on how you can live *above* your circumstances, and a plan whereby you can begin to become the woman, wife, and mother that you long to be!

THE BEAUTIFUL BLUEPRINT

Chapter Two

In a survey taken recently of 250 men and women to ascertain the most influential person in their lives, 212 of the 250 replied they had been most influenced by a woman.[1] Many times it was a wife or mother, but teachers, grandmothers, and Sunday School workers also appeared on the list! We all have heard that "the hand that rocks the cradle rules the world," but did you know that when Abraham Lincoln said that, he added, "And all that I am or hope to be I owe to my angel mother"?

We have been conditioned by today's advertising to respond instantly to the word *housewife* with the word *drudgery*. You know the scene in the magazine ad: exhausted woman dressed like Miss Rummage Sale 1956 slouched over an ironing board with six small children and the family dog wrapped around her ankles, and a pot boiling over on the stove. This is accompanied by a comforting message that after a grueling day in the home we can always take Excedrin to kill the pain, Nytol to calm us down, or Geritol to pep us up.

Partly as a result of this conditioning, many of us are now questioning ourselves, our roles, and life in general. And many of us are frustrated. One woman told me she could not wait until her four children were all in school so she could go out and contribute something to society. Every day she longed for them to go to bed so she could do something constructive for someone.

Isn't there more to being a wife and mother than refold-

wels that husbands fold wrong, keeping the static out of the family underwear, and getting kids to Little League on time? There is much more, and the much more is exciting! We've been brainwashed into believing the life of a wife and mother consists entirely of the "Three Cs": *cooking, cleaning,* and *car pooling.*

Remember, there are many frustrated wives, just as there are frustrated engineers, airline pilots, and karate instructors. But the frustration does not stem from the nature of the work; rather, it comes from the boredom inevitable in any job we do poorly or with little imagination.

A *creative counterpart* is more than just a helper. She is a wife who, having chosen (or finding herself in) the vocation of wife and mother, decides to learn and grow in all the areas of this role and to work as hard as if she were aiming for the presidency of a corporation.

Functioning as a professional in all areas of marriage is the essence of being a *creative counterpart*. Let's look at one such *creative counterpart* described many years ago by King Solomon in his ancient biblical monograph called Proverbs. There are many outstanding and godly women throughout the Bible, but Prov. 31:29 says of this one, "Many women have done excellently but you surpass them all" (RSV). Who is this woman who has done more than Deborah, the military advisor, than Ruth, the woman of constancy, than Queen Esther, who risked her life for her people? She is a wife and mother like you and me!

A study of this proverb reveals that verses 10 through 31 are a description of the virtuous woman. This passage is designed to show women what kind of wives they should be and to show men what kind of women they should choose to marry. It is also an acrostic poem; each of the twenty-two verses begins with a letter of the Hebrew alphabet in successive order, making it a literary as well as a spiritual masterpiece.

An excellent wife, who can find? (v. 10, NASB).

The word *excellent* means "a woman of strength." [2] It is the same word used to describe the character of Israel's judges, indicating that they were able and well-qualified for the business to which they were called—God-fearing men of truth. So it follows that a virtuous woman is one who is able and qualified for her profession, with command of her own spirit and able to manage others. She is a woman of resolution who, having chosen godly principles, is firm and faithful to them.[3] "Who can find her?" indicates that such a woman is very rare.

For her worth is far above jewels (v. 10, NASB).

The value of jewels, like that of people, depends on whether they are made by God or made by humans. This woman is a product of God's wisdom and skill. She has been fashioned within—as well as without—by God and has the priceless qualities only a godly woman can have. Her husband knows from experience how priceless she is. What would your husband trade you for right now? A few moments of peace and quiet? Or would he not trade you for the Hope Diamond?

The heart of her husband trusts in her,
And he will have no lack of gain (v. 11, NASB).

Trust is a major ingredient in marriage. The husband of this kind of wife trusts her conduct, her behavior in company. He knows she will always be loyal and never betray him.

Several years ago, when Jody and I were working in a campus ministry, I was gathering some material for teaching girls on "The Christian View of Sex, Love, and Marriage." I asked Jody what he appreciated most in me as a wife, and in his logical way he replied, "Your faithfulness." "Faithfulness?" I thought, "How dull!" His explanation made me appreciate him more than ever. "The most important thing to a man is to know that the woman he loves is on his team," he said. "If the rest of the world calls him a fool and deserts him, she'll be there beside him."

There is a trust relationship between the woman in Proverb 31 and her husband. Some have said that this trust could also apply to her husband's confidence in her ability to manage the household affairs: he knows she is competent and that when he arrives home at six, the home and family will not be in chaos but in order. Which does your husband find when he walks in the door?

The phrase "he will have no lack of gain" is extremely interesting. The word translated "gain" refers to the booty taken after a war—jewels, gold, and other costly items fought for and regarded as highly desirable.[4] The phrase says this woman's husband is so happy with her that he has no desire for all the wealth of the world: "Who needs money when I've got you?"

She does him good and not evil
All the days of her life (v. 12, NASB).

This trustworthy woman would never do anything to bring dishonor to her husband's name. She would not confide to her best friend how he has hurt her or get a laugh at the bridge table by listing his faults. Her own conduct is above reproach.

"All the days of her life" suggests her commitment to him is a decision of her will (not emotion) to stand by his side forever, regardless of what happens to them. Today the most common practice is to love your husband and do him good until problems come, and then it's every man for himself! "You live your life and I'll live mine. You do your thing and I'll do mine, and as long as they mesh it's beautiful, but as soon as they grate, we'll split!" In contrast, 1 Cor. 13:7 says love endures all things. The model wife of Proverb 31 makes a commitment to do good to her husband all the days of her life.

Paul says to the Corinthians, "Dearly beloved, we do all things for your edifying" (building them up and helping them grow in Christ). The excellent wife applies this to her husband and treats him with this attitude: "Dearly beloved, I do all things for your edifying," meaning she considers every word and action and then does and says only that which will build him up and help him.

> She looks for wool and flax,
> And works with her hands in delight (v. 13, NASB).

This phrase indicates that the excellent wife of King Solomon's day made clothing for her family with pleasure. The King James Version reads, "worketh willingly with her hands." The word *willing* got to me: there are many things in a woman's world (as well as in a man's world) that are not super-exciting! Maybe the housewife on TV is ecstatic because Lysol Basin Tub & Tile Cleaner gets her bathroom sparkling clean or because Mop 'n Glow makes her tingly all over, but somehow these products don't give me the same overjoyed feeling! In fact, I don't even remotely like cleaning the bathtub. But God doesn't say I have to have tingles; He says I am to do everything heartily as unto the Lord. We are to have a willing attitude and do everything in our home with pleasure because we are doing it for the people God has given us to love.

Are you willing to work hard, or do you look for excuses to avoid unpleasant tasks? I have a friend who is very depressed and unhappy. I truly believe one of the main causes of her depression is that she will not do anything that takes work. This verse tells us it is our *attitude* that counts, not whether we sew or cook gourmet meals, but that we work with *willing* hands.

> She is like merchant ships;
> She brings her food from afar (v. 14, NASB).

The good wife shops around to supply the needs of her home, investigating many possible sources. She hunts for bargains, going the extra mile to provide the best for her family.

> She rises also while it is still night,

> And gives food to her household,
> And portions to her maidens (v. 15, NASB).

In Solomon's time, the wife got up before the others in her household to start preparing and cooking the day's food and to plan and assign tasks to her maids. But I believe she was up early for another reason, too: to prepare herself spiritually as well as physically for the day's demands. The Amplified Bible translates it like this, "She rises while yet it is night and gets through communion with her God, spiritual food for her household." She knew if we say "good morning" to God first, our "good mornings" to everyone else will be better.

Jody and I had an inside joke about this verse. He would say, "Honey, when are you going to rise while it is still night like the excellent wife?" And I would reply, "Whenever I see the maids coming in the door!"

There are two ways that a day in the Dillow home can begin. The first way is for me to sleep through the alarm, finally drag my tired body out of bed, throw on my robe, rush into the girls' room, and tell them to hurry or they will be late. Then I scurry into Tommy's room, quickly dress him, and race to the kitchen to do all the things I should have done the night before. Finally, I throw breakfast on the table just in time for us to gulp down our food while I repeatedly encourage everyone to hurry. By the end of breakfast everyone is bickering, and I am wondering why the family is so nervous and uptight!

The second way is for me to be up before my family, dressed and with a smile on my face, talking with the Lord about the day and giving it to Him. After spending time with Him, cheerfully I go into Joy and Robin's room and kiss them both and awaken them. Then I proceed to Tommy's room to awaken him and help him get dressed.

Since the dishwasher was emptied, lunches made, and the table set the night before, making breakfast is a breeze. Everyone eats and is out the door with a smile. Of course there are days that fall somewhere in between these two extremes, but my family has said they much prefer the second way!

She considers a field and buys it;
From her earnings she plants a vineyard (v. 16, NASB).

She is an intelligent woman, and in her spare time she is a business woman. "Consider" stands out to me, since I occasionally have trouble saying the important word no. This prudent woman weighs each decision before assuming a new responsibility. We are asked to become involved in many activities, and unless we know our priorities and where we can contribute the most, we can easily become overextended. I am learning not to say yes immediately to every worthwhile activity, but instead to ask for time to think and pray about my decision.

She girds herself with strength,
And makes her arms strong (v. 17, NASB).

This is not figurative language; a modern paraphrase might be, "She diets and exercises to keep herself fit!" Being physically flabby contributes to flabbiness in our emotional and spiritual life as well as in our family and social relationships. I find when I'm in good physical condition I have more energy, am more mentally alert, and am more pleasant to be around.

She senses that her gain is good;
Her lamp does not go out at night (v. 18, NASB).

In Solomon's day, in a well-ordered house a lamp burned all night as a sign of life; its extinction signaled calamity.[5] This excellent wife spends her time profitably and sometimes continues her work into the night. As a result of her hard work, she sees success and satisfaction.

She stretches out her hands to the distaff,
And her hands grasp the spindle (v. 19, NASB).

Applying herself to the work of spinning, she does it with

skill. She is characterized by faithfulness. Whatever she does, she does skillfully, making the most of her abilities and talents. The emphasis is not on expertise but on attitude. Has your husband asked you to help him fix the car by turning the skeeziz spring counterclockwise with the gorilla grips? So it's unfamiliar to you—do it anyway (never mind the grease) with willing hands to the best of your ability.

> She extends her hand to the poor:
> And she stretches out her hands to the needy (v. 20, NASB).

She has so much love to give that it doesn't stop with her family. Her hands are continually outstretched to anyone in need.

Not long ago I spoke to a group of doctors' wives on the subject of "The Reality of Christianity in a Woman's World." Afterwards a smartly dressed woman approached me and said, "I think it's nice that you talk about a relationship with God, but what do you contribute to society? Do you ever go down into the ghetto to really help people?"

I replied, "God has given me a husband and three small children, and they come first in my life. Because of them I don't go to the ghetto, but I don't have to! There are so many needs in my neighborhood that I don't have to step one foot beyond it."

I live in an ordinary, average American neighborhood of young families, and inside a few square blocks there are people who are divorced, separated, or together but fighting, children with special problems, young mothers battling depression and bitterness, people who are sick—all people in need. How can we think the ghetto is the only place people have problems? I can contribute to society by remaining right where I am! The key is first to put your hand in God's. Tell Him you're available and willing to give of yourself, and ask Him to show you where you can help. I'm certain He'll answer by opening your eyes to a situation in which you can stretch out your hands to someone who needs you.

She is not afraid of the snow for her household.
For all her household are clothed with scarlet (v. 21, NASB).

"Scarlet clothing" refers to clothing of the best quality. And not only are these clothes of good quality; the excellent wife takes good care of them, too. We could paraphrase it like this: "Her family has clean shirts to put on in the morning and require not buttons to be sewed on while they stand waiting!"

She makes coverings for herself;
Her clothing is fine linen and purple (v. 22, NASB).

This doesn't mean she wears dressy clothing to scrub floors, but that she chooses garments that enhance her appearance. How hard do you try to appear attractive for your husband? Even the jeans you wear to clean the bathroom can fit well and be worn with a blouse he likes. As one woman put it, "MRS in front of your name does not mean *miserable rut of sloppiness!*"

Her husband is known in the gates,
When he sits among the elders of the land (v. 23, NASB).

Here the author of the proverb abruptly begins talking about the husband. It may seem strange this reference to the husband was put here, plopped right in the middle of all this praise of the excellent wife, with no apparent relationship to surrounding verses. But look closer. It's clear the author is saying, "Because of the quality of his wife, the husband is known in the gates. Because of her excellence, he is not only rich but important and famous."

She makes linen garments and sells them,
And supplies belts to the tradesmen (v. 24, NASB).

Where did she get the money to buy land? From her business venture of making and selling her handiwork. Today this would perhaps be comparable to a part-time job done in the home.

Strength and dignity are her clothing,
And she smiles at the future (v. 25, NASB).

Although a woman may be attired in becoming clothing, when people see her walk into a room their eye is not captured by her dress but by the quality of her presence. Something beneath the exterior is apparent—a calm and gentle spirit produced by strength of character and dignity of manner. "Strength" indicates she has resources to survive trials, quite the opposite of the "helpless honey" who goes all to pieces under stress. "She smiles at the future" suggests she relies on her inner strength and her adequate economic position to carry her securely through any future difficulties.

She opens her mouth in wisdom,
And the teaching of kindness is on her tongue (v. 26, NASB).

In the Amplified Bible this verse is translated, "She opens her mouth with skillful and godly Wisdom, and in her tongue is the law of kindness." Wisdom is equated with skill—she has skillful counsel and wise instruction for others. Living life according to God's principles is a skill, just like playing the piano or sewing. The excellent woman works hard at developing this special skill, and it shows in the way she lives, in the words she speaks, and in the counsel she gives to others.

Just think for a minute what our homes and our world would be like if each of us applied this verse to our everyday lives. Would there be a difference in your relationship with your husband and children if you only opened your mouth with wisdom and if the law of kindness were on your tongue? Have you ever noticed the difference between the intonation you reserve for your friends and the one you use with your family? It's so easy to give our best to comparative strangers and toss our family the leftovers.

One young mother of eight came into the room and found all her children bickering. She gently admonished them, "Children, don't you know the Bible says we should be kind to one another?" Her eldest, who was nine, looked thoughtfully around the room and replied, "But Mommy, there's nobody here but the family!"

She looks well to the ways of her household,
And does not eat the bread of idleness (v. 27, NASB).

She supervises all that goes on in her home. The wife of
Solomon's day may have had her maids, and today's wife
her modern conveniences or her cleaning lady, but both are
instructed to be on top of what goes on in their household.
The excellent wife is a professional in her job and is willing
to work hard at managing and supervising.

Her children rise up and bless her; (v. 28a, NASB).

The term *rise up* means "to go into public life." [6] As the
children of a good mother grow up, they become a testimony
to their mother by their lives and their words, and they bless
her for their early training. Children today are rising up and
calling their mothers all sorts of things, but few are calling
them blessed!

Her husband also, and he praises her, saying:
"Many daughters have done nobly,
But you excel them all" (vv. 28–29, NASB).

I could have plaques on my wall inscribed with flowery
words of praise from the Chamber of Commerce, the Ladies'
Missionary Society, the PTA, the Girl Scouts, and my sorority
alumnae group, but what would these mean in comparison
with honor bestowed by the people who know me best?
When people who live with you day in and day out praise
you, it means something! They have seen you at your worst
as well as your best. They will praise your inner qualities,
not your outward achievements. A friend of mine gave this
humorous description of marriage: "It's very humbling to
known that there's one other person in the world who knows
what a rat you are!"

The reason the excellent woman is so excellent is found in
verse 30:

Charm is deceitful and beauty is vain,
But a woman who fears the Lord, she shall be praised
(NASB).

A modern paraphrase might be, "Charm is often deceiving, hiding an ugly personality, and beauty is only skin deep, but a woman who fears God is truly charming and lovely." The virtuous woman first and foremost fears and worships God. She is trustworthy, industrious, faithful, charitable, strong, wise, cautious, compassionate, generous, kind, and more! Does this description overwhelm you? Do you want to be this kind of woman, but feel you'll never even get started? We'll continue to be overwhelmed if we keep looking at ourselves, because then we see only our own inadequacies.

The key to becoming a *creative counterpart* is a vital relationship with God. He promises to make each of us into the kind of woman He wants us to be (Phil. 1:6). He doesn't say it will be easy, but He guarantees results!

GOD'S GAME PLAN

Chapter Three

How does this excellent woman come to be? Through the centuries women have read about the woman in Proverb 31 and have wanted to be like her. But how? We have spoken of her hard work and diligence in learning to live life by God's principles, but we have also said she is a product of God's working within her. So who does it? If you want to become a *creative counterpart*, will God do it through you or will you have to do it? These are the extremes people have often tended toward in viewing the work of the Holy Spirit in their lives.

I MUST DO IT ALL (or The Guilt Trip)

One extreme is the overemphasis on the part of the individual. Susan is such a wife. She thinks people are responsible for their own spiritual progress, so she reads the commandments of Scripture and then sets herself a program to obey them. After reading a book on marriage or attending a seminar she sets about doing everything she can to live out the principles. The problem is she falls into a frustrating cycle. The harder she tries the more she fails. The more she fails the guiltier she feels. The guiltier she feels the harder she tries. And round and round she goes, seemingly trapped in a life of frustration. She has reduced the New Testament to a set of rules or laws, and she does the same with the books and seminars she attends. Because she is unclear as to exactly how God will help her in her struggle, she is trapped in a cycle.

Books, seminars,
New Testament exhortations
↓
Trying Hard

Feelings
of Guilt   Failure

The New Testament exhortations to be an excellent wife seem a dreadful burden. She views them as external laws to be obeyed. She constantly compares her life with those of other women who seem to be doing so much better a job of being a wife than she. Her experience with the "law" was similar to that of the apostle Paul, "I do not know what I am doing. For what I want to do I do not do, but what I hate I do" (Rom. 7:15, NIV).

Susan's problem is complicated because her husband has severe emotional problems. He spends much of his time in deep depressions, and he takes his frustration out on her and the children. The more she tries to be what she "is supposed to be" the more she seems to be slapped in the face. He spends money irresponsibly, checks bounce all over town, his life style is immoral, and he is affecting the children. All her attempts to love him are rebuffed with indifference, hurt, and insensitivity. Emotionally she is drained, but she feels guilty, because she is unable to respond as the lady who taught the seminar told her she should. Thus the guilt mounts.

GOD DOES IT ALL (or the Mystical Takeover)
Mary, on the other hand, thinks God will do it all. Her motto is, "Let go and let God!" She believes if she just trusts Jesus, the Holy Spirit will do all the work through her. God alone will remove her inconsistencies.

She talks very spiritually and really sounds like a candidate for sainthood, but her husband can't stand to live with her. He is not a Christian and is highly offended by her "spiritual" tone. Her home is usually a mess, she is not a good wife, and her children are among the most undisciplined on the block. She is just "trusting Jesus" to take over and do the work through her. To all the world she sounds like a victorious Christian. She says all the right words and talks in glowing terms of how the Lord works through her in this or that circumstance.

Inside, however, Mary is miserable. She knows in her heart that her life does not match her glowing spiritual talk. As a result she is inwardly frustrated, because no matter how often she speaks of "God doing it through her" God doesn't seem to be doing much through her. She sincerely wants to be a better wife and mother, but her Christianity isn't producing the expected results. It has never dawned on her that part of the problem could be her view of the Christian life. Therefore, she is always looking for the "secret" of the Christian life, and she has a special focus on some unique or unusual manifestations of the Holy Spirit. But the result is that while she sits waiting for God to work she not only becomes frustrated and guilt-ridden, just like Susan, but she also has started spending large quantities of time and energy searching for the "secret" of the Spirit-filled life.

A young woman with Mary's perspective once told me she knew God did not want her to get up and have a devotional time in the morning because, as she explained, "I told God if He wanted me to get up and have a devotional time then He could get me up at six-thirty, and I didn't wake up until seven-thirty." When I asked her if she had an alarm clock, she replied that she didn't do anything unless God motivated her. God did it all, and she was to do only what she felt He was motivating her to do.

THE BALANCE: 100 Percent + 100 Percent

Philippians 2:12–13 puts it all in focus: "Work out your

salvation with fear and trembling; for it is God who is at work in you, both to will and to work for His good pleasure" (NASB). The Living Bible states it this way: "You must be even more careful to do the good things that result from being saved, obeying God with deep reverence, shrinking back from all that might displease him. For God is at work within you, helping you want to obey him, and then helping you do what he wants."

Paul is instructing the Philippians to do what God would want *because* of His unconditional love and forgiveness toward them. They are to obey, not wait for God to make them want to obey, because of what He did for them in giving them eternal and abundant life in Jesus. They are to do the positive and shrink back from the negative. And the reason they will be able to do this is that God will be constantly at work within them through the Holy Spirit, helping them *want* to obey and then helping them do all that God requires.

This is the balance. It's not 100 percent God or 100 percent me; neither is it 50 percent God and 50 percent me. It's 100 percent God and 100 percent me—both of us doing our 100 percent together. Our relationship with God is much like our relationship with our husbands: each partner must give 100 percent.

GOD'S 100 PERCENT

However, in a marriage relationship there is the possibility that either partner can fail, hurt the other, decide to leave, or forsake his commitment. In our relationship with God only one partner can fail, hurt or forsake, and I guarantee you it's not God! Let's look at all He has already done for us and what He is doing for us every day.

NEW POSITION

"He made Him who knew no sin to be sin on our behalf, that we might become the righteousness of God in Him" (2 Cor. 5:21, NASB). We sinners have been declared righteous! We stand in grace; we are justified. If you know Jesus Christ as your personal Savior and Lord, there is nothing you can do to increase or decrease God's love for you. If I were to read my Bible twelve hours and do twenty-nine good deeds today, God would not love me any more than He did before. (He would be *shocked* if I read my Bible for twelve hours, but it wouldn't increase His love for me!) We might interpret "justified" as being "just as if I'd never sinned." God does not receive those who are justified on the basis of how well they live up to the beautiful blueprint in Proverb 31, but completely on the merits of His Son.

Have you at times felt like a failure as a wife? I know I have! What a comfort to know God does not accept me on the basis of how well I succeed in doing what He wants me to do. Because of Christ's death, every barrier to full fellowship with God has been removed. I stand totally accepted, not on the basis of how I perform but on the basis of Christ's merits. I stand before God in Jesus' name and not on my success.

NEW PERSON

To regenerate is to endow with new life and vigor, to renew spiritually. This is exactly what Paul is describing in 2 Cor. 5:17, "Therefore if any man is in Christ, he is a new creature; the old things passed away; behold, new things have come" (NASB).

God has given us a new nature, resulting in a new motivation toward godliness. This is proven by the very fact of your desire to understand what God wants you to understand about being His woman in the home. It's what Peter calls longing for the pure milk of the Word (1 Pet. 2:2) and is characteristic of everyone who knows Christ personally. Thank God He has given you this desire! That desire comes from Him and in itself is evidence of His working in your life. Those outside of Christ know of no such desire. That is one reason the national divorce rate is close to one out of two now. God has given you the desire to be the kind of *creative counterpart* that will result in you and your family living the maximum life. Praise Him for what He has already done!

NEW POWER

How would you like to be "set apart as holy, to be consecrated"? Guess what? God has already promised this for you as He progressively makes you more like Himself. At the moment you received Jesus Christ as your Savior, God gave you the Holy Spirit, who will teach you the deep things of God, will guide you into all truth, and will give you power to live the Christian life. God knows we could never live it on our own.

God has done much for us in the past, yet it is easy to start focusing on our circumstances and to forget His faithfulness. Recently I was reading through Genesis and Exodus and was again overwhelmed at the marvelous miracles God performed for the Israelites. I read of the ten plagues He brought upon Egypt to convince Pharaoh to release the people, and then of their journey that brought them to the Red Sea.

Imagine being one of that company milling in panic beside the water, Pharaoh's army in hot pursuit. The only way you can escape death by the sword is death by drowning. Then, as the sun goes down, a strong wind sweeps in and parts the waters right before your eyes, and a path becomes visible through the middle of the sea! A gasp from the people behind you causes you to whirl around to see a gigantic pillar of fire that has appeared between you and the Egyptian chariots. All through the night the fiery glow illuminates the camp and the path that is drying on the seabed, while on the other side of the pillar the Egyptians have been plunged into total darkness, where they wait for the morning light to renew their chase.

With the first rays of the dawn Moses gives the command.

Hesitating for a moment between the towering walls of sea water on either side of the path and the clanks and cries and whines from the Egyptian camp, you move forward, down onto the now-solid seabed and across onto the other side. As the last of your people reach safety, your pursuers rush down onto the same path through the sea! Panic grips you again, but then you see Moses stretch out his hand over the sea, and with a mighty roar the walls of water come crashing down on the Egyptians. Their heavy armor and chariots pull them to the bottom, and the waters close over them. In a few moments, no trace of your enemies remains. God has delivered you! You'll never doubt God again after such a string of miracles!

Or will you? We humans forget so quickly! History tells us that just three days later the Israelites began to grumble to Moses because of their circumstances.

It's easy for us to think, "How could they?" But a look at our own lives shows us how quick we are to forget all God has done for us. We are continually exhorted throughout Scripture to "remember what God has done." I'm convinced that if we do, it will make a tremendous difference in our lives, as we remember God has not only justified and re-generated us, but has given us Himself as our companion. He has not left us alone to live the Christian life, but has actually come to live within us to empower each of us to be a creative counterpart.

NEW PROMISES

Now, how can this power be experienced in one's life? The answer to that leads us into a consideration of what God promises to do. We must not only see what He has already done, but we must claim by faith what He promises to do.

HE'LL NEVER LEAVE US

I have been told that there are over seven thousand promises in the Bible. One of my favorites is found in Heb.

13:5: "I will never desert you, nor will I ever forsake you" (NASB). Sounds good, doesn't it? But it's even better when you understand the full meaning. In the Greek language, in which the New Testament was written, there is what is called a triple negative. It is used when the author wants something to be extremely emphatic. This is the only verse in the New Testament in which this triple negative is used, and literally translated it reads: "I will not, I will not, I will not, in any degree leave you helpless, nor forsake you, nor relax my hold on you, assuredly not." Now that's what I call a promise! And there are 6,999 more!

TO MAKE US CHRISTLIKE

Note Paul's familiar statement, "And we know that in all things God works for the good of those who love him, who have been called according to his purpose" (Rom. 8:28, NIV). Too frequently we stop there, ignoring the next verse. What is His purpose? "For those God foreknew he also predestined *to be conformed to the likeness of his Son,* that he might be the firstborn among many brothers" (Rom. 8:29, NIV).

True, all works together for good, but what is good? *Good* is here defined as Christ-likeness, as possessing the fruit of the Holy Spirit in one's life. This fruit is described in Gal. 5:22,23 as love, joy, peace, patience, kindness, goodness, faithfulness, gentleness, and self-control. Wouldn't you like to possess these qualities? According to Rom. 8:28–29, God is working in all the trials and joys of your marriage for this ultimate purpose, to develop in your life these beautiful qualities.

Consider Rom. 5:2, "And we rejoice in the hope of the glory of God. Not only so, but we also rejoice in our sufferings, because we know that suffering produces perseverance; perseverance, character; and character, hope. And hope does not disappoint us, because God has poured out his love into our hearts by the Holy Spirit, whom he has given us" (NIV).

Have you considered your present situation in the light of God's eternal purpose? Often the very things we resist and resent are God's special tools to fashion us into the image of His son. Even though we may not see the outcome now of a problem child, an insensitive husband, a financial or sexual problem, we do see that God has not abandoned us, and we can be sure He has a definite, loving purpose in allowing this into our lives. This perspective is fundamental to experiencing the power of the Holy Spirit.

NO TEMPTATION TOO GREAT

"No temptation has overtaken you but such as is common to man; and God is faithful, who will not allow you to be tempted beyond what you are able; but with the temptation will provide the way of escape also, that you may be able to endure it" (1 Cor. 10:13, NASB). Each of us is at a different point in our life, each has a different husband, and some of us have problems in our personal lives or marriages we feel are too heavy, too insurmountable. God promises there is no temptation too great and that He will provide a way for each of us to endure it. Sometimes our problem is simply that we are not sincerely giving our troubles to the Lord and seeking His face, but are trying to go it alone.

GOD'S CONSTANT CONCERN

"Casting all your anxiety upon Him, because He cares for you" (1 Pet. 5:7, NASB). God wants us to cast all those problems and worries on His strong shoulders because He loves us and is concerned for us. How do you do this? By choice of will. You decide that the problem should be given to the Lord and simply *will it* into His hands. Since we are so prone to unbelief, within two minutes of giving the problem to Him we usually find the old fears, doubts, and worries returning. It is as if we have given the problem to Him and then said, "Lord, let me take it back for a little while. I'm not confident you can really handle it. I think it will help the situation if I worry and fret about it for another day or so."

Give it to Him and leave it in His hands. When the doubts return every two minutes, rededicate the problem to Him with another choice of will, and another, and another, and another until you have finally come to feel that you have trusted it into His hands. This may take several days or even weeks before you are truly able to leave it. This is part of the struggle of the Christian life. This is why the writer to the Hebrews paradoxically exhorts us, "Let us, therefore, make *every effort* to enter that rest" (Heb. 4:11, NIV). It takes *effort* to enter into rest!

We see the balance of the Christian life again in Phil. 4:13, "I can do all things through Him [Christ] who strengthens me" (NASB). *I* can do all things through *Christ* who strengthens me. God has promised to be faithful to us, never to leave us, to give us the power and strength to live the Christian life. So how can we experience what God promises to do?

MAN'S 100 PERCENT

It can be summed up in one little verse. First Corinthians says, "Moreover it is required . . . that a man be found faithful" 4:2, KJV). The world says, "It is required of a man that he should be found successful, rich, famous, and attractive." But God requires only one thing: that we be faithful!

Does this call to your mind the parable of the talents in Matthew 25? Jesus tells the story of a man who was about to go on a long trip. He called his servants and gave to one of them five silver coins (called talents), to another two talents, and to a third one talent.

Upon his return he again called the three servants to him, this time to evaluate what they had done with what had been given them. Discovering that the first servant had invested his five talents and now had ten he praised him: "Well done, good and faithful slave; you were faithful with a few things, I will put you in charge of many things, enter into the joy of your master." The slave who had been given five talents had also doubled his money, and was given the same praise.

But the third slave had buried his one talent and had not multiplied it. He received not praise but great wrath from his master. The issue here is not how many talents you have but how you use them. Are you a faithful servant? This is man's part. It is to trust and obey. When we do, we begin to experience God working in us.

TRUST

Trust in what? In a word? It is trust in a person—Jesus Christ. You are trusting in Him for what He has already done and for what He promises to do. If you want to experience the release of the Spirit in your life, you must begin to relate every circumstance and situation in your marriage to these promises. They must become the way you look at life. That would begin by at least having them memorized!

The next time your husband hurts you, it is no longer to be viewed as an unnecessary and irritating pain, but it now becomes attached to God's promises to make you Christlike by working through that hurt. The proper response is "In everything give thanks: for this is the will of God in Christ Jesus concerning you" (1 Thess. 5:18, KJV).

We are told, "No discipline seems pleasant at the time, but painful. Later on, however, it produces a harvest of righteousness and peace for those who have been trained by it" (Heb. 12:11, NIV). That harvest of righteousness is not seen at the time. It is hoped for. "Now faith is being sure of what we hope for and certain of what we do not see" (Heb. 11:1, NIV).

Sometimes the problems are so great that it seems like total blindness to continue to trust. Yet God rejoices in the woman who trusts Him when all the circumstances seem impossible. Consider Abraham, "By faith Abraham, when called to go to a place he would later receive as his possession, obeyed and went, even though he did not know where he was going" (Heb. 11:8, NIV). He trusted God with naked faith! God promised him a land and a seed even though all he owned was a tent and a piece of the land just large enough to bury his wife on.

By faith, we must claim what God has promised as if it were ours already. How is this done? By coming to the Lord in prayer and verbally claiming the promise, by thanking Him for the promise and expressing your trust in Him that he is going to fulfill the promise *in His good and perfect time.* He knows what is best for us and will therefore see to it that the promises are fulfilled in the most perfect way.

We do the possible by faith, trusting God to do the impossible. Let me give you an illustration of how I found this to work in my life.

Early one morning last winter I was driving the first-grade car pool to school. It was raining unexpectedly and fiercely. The streets were slick, I was tired, and the three children were quarreling in the back seat. (There seems to be something about car pooling that brings out the fighting instincts in all small children!)

As I was driving down the winding road I was meditating on God's part and my part. Silently in prayer I told God that I hated to drive in the rain but that I wanted to do all I could —I wanted to be faithful to do my part. I told Him I would do all I could to drive safely but that I knew only He could keep me and my three precious passengers safe.

I spoke to the children and the bickering stopped. I held the steering wheel tightly, turned on the lights, drove slowly, and stayed as alert as possible. Thirty seconds after I uttered my prayer I had a blowout. Just ahead on the shoulder of the road was a space just big enough for my car—the only place within a mile where it was possible to pull off the road. And would you believe that directly across the street was the only gas station within miles? The attendant met me and the children at the door with, "Boy, lady, you sure are lucky! You could have had a bad accident!"

Lucky? No. Blessed? Definitely! Blessed by a loving Father who wants us to be faithful to do our part, and who over and over is faithful to do His part.

OBEY

The second aspect of faithfulness is consistent obedience. We must not be like Mary who is only "trusting" Jesus and never really obeying him, nor are we to be like Susan, who is so totally focused on obedience that she becomes guilt-ridden. We must trust and obey. That is our 100 percent.

Take another look at the story of Lazarus (John 11). The brother of Mary and Martha and the beloved friend of Jesus had died and been buried for four days when Jesus arrived at his home in Bethany. Mary and Martha told Jesus through their tears that if he had been there, Lazarus would not have died. After asking them to show him where they had laid Lazarus, Jesus directed them to roll back the large stone that secured the grave opening, and in a loud voice commanded the dead man to come out. When Lazarus appeared in the doorway, still wrapped in the grave clothes, Jesus ordered the people to unwrap him.

Do you see the principle in this story? Jesus asked the people to do all the things they could do: show him the grave, roll away the stone, unwrap the grave clothes. And Jesus did what they could not do: raise Lazarus from the dead!

I have seen Christians literally sit waiting for God to motivate them. Wives have told me that God has just not given them a feeling of love for their husband. God *does* give motivation, God *does* give feelings, but usually they come as a result of our obedience to Him. We must first make a decision of our will ("I will be the kind of person God would have me be") and then *act,* step out in obedience to God. God promises He is at work within us doing His part. And that's exciting!

It seems that God really wants us to understand how this works, because He has given us one whole book of the Bible that shows this concept as clearly as if He had painted us a picture. If you've never studied the book of Ephesians, get out your Bible and begin now! I guarantee you'll be excited!

Notice that the first three chapters of Paul's letter to the church at Ephesus are a description of all the glorious things God has done and is doing for us. This first half of the book is a beautiful treatise on the love and grace of God toward us in Jesus Christ.

Do you notice anything missing from these chapters? Right! There is not one command given. Paul is a good command-giver, so this does seem strange.

But hold on; here come chapters four, five, and six. In them we are given thirty-three commands—thirty-three things that we are to do in response to what God has already done! God has done His 100 percent and has continued to be faithful to us, and now we are to do our 100 percent. It's as if Paul is saying to us, "Just look at all God has given you. See His unconditional love and acceptance of you, bask in His grace and realize all you've been given, and *then* respond. Respond by giving of yourself, by exerting your will, and putting feet on the word *obey.* Respond by going, doing, and being what God has commanded."

A LIFELONG PROCESS

Learning to obey and to trust is a process that takes repetition and discipline. Paul says, "*Discipline* yourself for the purpose of godliness" (1 Tim. 4:7, NASB). Godliness is the product of *training.* It was said of Jesus, "Although He was a son, He *learned obedience* from the things which he suffered" (Heb. 5:8, NASB).

God wants to make you a *creative counterpart* to your husband. He wants the finished product to be His work. "For we are God's workmanship, created in Christ Jesus to do good works, which God prepared in advance for us to do." (Eph. 2:10, NIV). God has given us the Holy Spirit to empower, strengthen, and guide. That power is released as we set our will to obey while simultaneously trusting that it is God's will to work in us. Our trust comes from a certain knowledge of our own inability to live it; our obedience comes from the confidence that if we obey and trust He will fulfill his promise, and His Spirit will mold us into His image.

It is a process that takes a lifetime. If God wants to grow a cabbage, He can do it in a few months, but if He wants to grow an oak tree, He has decreed it will take Him a lifetime. God is trying to produce oak-tree Christians—Christians with deep roots, who have learned obedience, who have "strong trunks" that are not easily swayed by the winds or trials. Settle on his ultimate objective and purpose in your heart to be faithful to trust and obey now! That's our part. His part is, through the power of the Holy Spirit, to do what He has promised in His own way and in His own time.

By now you may be protesting, "I thought this was a book on how to be a *creative counterpart.* You haven't been talking about my marriage but about my relationship to God! Maybe I picked up the wrong book!" You thought you were going to learn how to be creative, loving, organized, and all the other goodies that will make your marriage a love affair. You are! But in the process you will be bombarded with your responsibilities as a wife, mother, woman, and Christian, and that can be overwhelming. So first we need to focus on ourselves in the context of God and His faithfulness to us. Look at God, at how He is at work in your life, molding you, changing you, encouraging you, helping you. God will never give up on you, even on those days when you wail, "I'll *never* be a *creative counterpart!*" God wants you to be a *creative counterpart.* He is there, and He will never leave you nor forsake you.

Now, armed with His promises, let's begin!

THE PRIORITY PLANNER

Chapter Four

Teach us to number our days,
That we may present to Thee a heart of wisdom (NASB).

A friend of mine took these words of Ps. 90:12 to heart and totaled up the number of days she would have left on earth if she lived to be seventy. She was thirty at the time, and discovered that the remaining forty years would give her 14,600 days. She was greatly challenged and motivated by this: forty years had seemed like a long time until she saw the time broken down into days and realized how swiftly life passes. She resolved then to live each day to the fullest. But as with so many of us, the zeal lasted for about a week, and then she forgot about it. When she remembered and again numbered her days, several years had passed and she discovered that she had only 12,000 days remaining! "Where did they go?" she asked herself. "What did I do with those 2,600 days?"

What *do* we do with our days? Our male counterparts always seem to know what they're doing with theirs. Men are generally more goal-oriented than women; a man usually has his life laid out before him and knows where he is heading: in five years he will be a division manager in his company, in ten years he will start his own business, and in fifteen he will make a million dollars!

How many women have plans like this? Most of us just let one day flow into the next and the days into weeks and the weeks into months, and before we know it another year has passed! Is New Year's Day a time of satisfied reflection for you, or are you like my neighbor, who remarked to me last January that she couldn't think of anything she had accomplished in the past year?

At the end of his life the apostle Paul was able to say, "I have fought the good fight, I have finished the race. . . . Now there is in store for me the crown of righteousness" (2 Tim. 4:7–8, NIV). Too many women approach the end of life and inwardly lament, "I've fought a mediocre fight as a wife and mother. I didn't run well in my race." What a tragedy! But you can do something about your own life *now*.

What is *your* goal in life? Do you even have one? Most of us don't think in terms of a lifetime; we're concerned about getting the laundry done on Monday and getting tonight's dinner on the table. Take a minute right now and write in one paragraph or less your life goal. I've thought a lot about this and have decided that, simply stated, my goal is to be a godly woman, to be all that God wants me to be as a woman, wife, and mother.

Sounds good on paper, doesn't it? But how am I going to fill this big order? Think for a minute with me. What areas of responsibility make up a woman's world? Write down your answer. I came up with the areas of children, husband, God, self, home, and a job or other outside activities. How are we going to organize these into priorities in order to live each day to the fullest and grow more like the excellent wife of Proverb 31?

PRIORITY #1 – GOD

But seek first His kingdom, and His righteousness; and all these things shall be added to you (Matt. 6:33, NASB).

Our relationship with God must come first. Why? Because we need God's perspective in every other area of our lives. We see this in His commands to us: "But seek first his kingdom and his righteousness, and all these things will be given to you as well" (Matt. 6:33, NIV) and "Jesus replied, 'Love the Lord your God with all your heart, with all your soul and with all your mind. This is the first and greatest commandment' " (Matt. 22:37, 38, NIV). God knows we need to spend time with Him to get to know Him and to learn His game plan for our lives.

One of the biggest and most common mistakes women make is to substitute *activity* for God for a *relationship* with Him. On the outside, we're busy running the holy hurdles, but on the inside our relationship with Christ is at a standstill.

I have always been able to identify with Martha in the New Testament. When Jesus comes to visit her and Mary and Lazarus, we find Mary sitting at his feet to learn from Him (Luke 10:3). Mary is mentioned five times in the New Testament, and each time we find her at the feet of Jesus. And then we see Martha. She's up scurrying around as many of us would be, preparing food, attending to the guests, tidying the house. Martha is the organizer. Martha's contributions *were* important, yet when she complained to Jesus that Mary was not helping her He replied that Mary had "chosen what is better."

Christ was not saying that organizing, cooking, and serving are not important. They are, and we can receive much joy from doing these things. Yet all the activity in the world will never give us the peace and joy of a vital relationship with Jesus Christ. We need to spend more time sitting at the feet of Jesus.

To know Jesus in a personal way, we need to zero in on four major areas:

TALKING WITH GOD

If I talked with Jody only between eleven and twelve on Sunday morning, how well would I know him? Prayer, talking with God, is vital in building an exciting relationship with Jesus Christ. First Thessalonians 5:18 says we are to pray without ceasing. No one can pray all the time! This verse describes an attitude of prayer. I think of it in this way: whenever my mind is disengaged (such as when I clean a bathtub), my thoughts can go to prayer instead of to resentment, anxiety, or frustration. I can thank God for my children as I load the dishwasher and ask His help while I'm driving the car pool to school.

Mark 2:5 describes Jesus getting up early to meet with His Father. This seems to indicate Christians need specific times of prayer with God as well as praying short prayers through the day. Prayer is hard work, so most of us avoid it. There are so many things to pray about that we're afraid if we ever got down on our knees we'd never get up!

An imaginative Christian friend took the days of the week and used them as guidelines for her prayer life. Using this pattern she feels everyone get prayed for!

Monday	— missionaries
Tuesday	— tasks
Wednesday	— wants and needs
Thursday	— thanksgiving
Friday	— friends
Saturday	— saints
Sunday	— sinners

"All right," you say. "But how do I do it? I don't think I can come up with enough churchy phrases to keep going!" Relax. God doesn't want a recital of the prayer book; He wants you to be yourself. He wants you to use the words you normally use in talking with your friends or with your husband. (Since he's your Father, you can even call Him "You" instead of "Thou"!) He also wants you to be specific. Instead of "Thank you for all my many blessings," why not try "Thank you for providing the extra money we needed to pay our medical bills this month."

God longs for you to bring to Him the things that have really made you happy or that really cause you concern. Nothing is too small for His attention, or out of His realm. Some of us think certain matters are inappropriate for His ears. One wife came to me seeking counsel about her sexual relationship with her husband. After some discussion I asked her if she had ever prayed about it. She recoiled in shock and gasped, "Oh, no! I don't talk to God about things like *that!*" How sadly ironic that we creatures of the Creator feel He wouldn't understand certain parts of our lives. Our heavenly Father knows us inside out and longs to talk with us about every detail of our existence.

LIKE NEWBORN BABES

We need to listen to God speak through the Scriptures as well as converse with Him in prayer. Peter says like newborn babies we are to "long for the pure milk of the word," in order that we may grow by taking it in (1 Pet. 2:2, NASB). Anyone who has experienced motherhood knows that a baby doesn't quietly and meekly request his milk, "if it wouldn't be too much trouble for you, please." He screams, he wails, he rages until the milk is within reach, and then he lunges for it in desperation and drinks ravenously. He acts as though he'll starve to death if you delay one second longer! This should be our attitude toward the Word! Nothing else will truly satisfy the hunger of our inner selves. Our problem is that we don't realize how hungry we are!

God also says His book will be a lamp for our feet and a light for our path. Everything we need to know about God, ourselves, and life has been written in God's love letter to us. "All Scripture is God-breathed and is useful for teaching, rebuking, correcting and training in righteousness, so that the man of God may be thoroughly equipped for every good work" (2 Tim. 3:16–17, NIV).

The rich truths of God's Word have been compared to gold in a mine, with the big problem being how to dig them out! Today we are blessed with an abundance of exciting study guides, Bible handbooks, and commentaries to help us with our investigation. Remember that these are only tools to aid you, and should not be substituted for your own deep inspection of the Word.

What are the results? As a mother I can give my children answers concerning life and death and heaven and eternity, as well as things in the here and now. My children will realize the importance of God's Word only as I answer their questions from it.

Recently a neighbor, the mother of two young boys, became ill and lay near death for several weeks. Our family prayed for her and tried to help the father and sons, but my seven-year-old daughter didn't want to pray for her and refused to talk about her illness. I wondered what I had done wrong to produce such a heartless child. Later that week, after teaching a seminar, I arrived home to find gifts my children had made for me. Among my daughter's drawings was a letter. It read, "Dear Mommy, I love you. I love you very much. I hope you never die. Love, Joy."

Her seeming lack of sensitivity was actually fear that her Mommy would also get sick and die. I took her in my arms and shared with her what God's Word said about life and death. We had talked about these things before, but now they took on real meaning. How I thanked God that I knew His Word and could give my children answers from Him! And how He has challenged me with the realizaton that I can give my children no more than I have myself.

INTO THE CLOSET

The best time to build your relationship with Christ through prayer and Bible study is during a devotional time. I know how many of us really struggle with this! We manage to carve out the time for maybe a week, and then we give up. I think one reason for our failure is that we set our goals too high: "I'll be up every morning at six!" I've tried this and by the third day I'm so exhausted that I can't even find the Bible, let alone study it!

God wants us to be realistic. Right now it is realistic for me to be up early three mornings a week to spend time with Him. The other days I have a quiet time while my children are resting. As they grow, I'll be able to get up early more mornings each week. Evaluate your life and set a goal that is realistic for you. Don't feel guilty if you read about some dear saint who gets up at five every morning to pray for her nine children! A devotional time is not a law but a relationship. Your relationship with the Savior will be different from everyone else's.

Your quiet time is a time for you to draw apart with God. It is a special time for you to talk over with Him the events of the day, your growth in Him, your concerns, your blessings. A quiet time is not a time to prepare your Sunday School lesson quietly. Neither is it a time to browse through a church magazine or even to write to your missionary.

It is a time set aside to deepen your knowledge of the Lord, to enrich your own personal relationship with Him, to fellowship with Him, to love Him, to worship Him, on a very personal basis. This quiet time each day is for YOUR OWN PERSONAL GROWTH in the Lord. No matter how old you are in the Lord or how closely you walk with Him, I feel this little time of intimate fellowship will always be necessary.

You may have a set time for it, or it may happen several times during the day. You may take five minutes, or five hours, as the Spirit and circumstances lead, but vital personal contact with the Lord is necessary, in order that you may have a constant inpouring of the life of Christ, that He may channel it through you to others. Do not ever feel you must stick to rules and regulations in order to achieve this. If you DESIRE to know Him better, the Holy Spirit will certainly lead you in your efforts, even if you never see any helps on the subject.[1]

FELLOWSHIP

What do you do when at age thirty-two you find yourself divorced and your children in your husband's custody? You could commit suicide, blame God, pity yourself, or eat yourself into obesity. Betty chose another path. Committing herself to Christ and trusting Him to work good out of tragedy, she sought help from other Christians.

"My Christian friends saw my need and fulfilled it to the point of self-sacrifice," she told me. "They believed in me as a person, accepted me as I was, but had a vision for what I could become. I had families to live with, brothers and sisters who provided my inner and outer needs."

Wilma's pain was physical. While a college student she discovered she had a serious illness and now lives with daily pain and discomfort. No one can help her physical pain, but the body of Christ has ministered to Wilma by reminding her of God's eternal perspective—a "ministry of reminding" her to apply God's truths to her daily walk. "Therefore, I shall always be ready to remind you of these things, even though you already know them, and have been established in the truth which is present with you" (2 Pet. 1:12, NASB).

Fellowship has a deeper meaning than mere friendship. The Greek word for fellowship is *koinonia* which means "sharing in common." We desperately need to share our Christian experience with others who believe and likewise allow them to share with us. "Under Christ's direction the whole body is fitted together perfectly and each part in its own special way helps the other parts, so that the whole body is healthy and growing and full of love" (Eph. 4:16, TLB).

In the body of Christ there is no age. Some of my richest fellowship has been with women twice my age, and encouragement and spiritual insight have often been given to me by my children.

I always longed for a sister, and God has given me special sisters in Christ to encourage, exhort and build me up. "And let us consider how to stimulate one another to love and good deeds" (Heb. 10:24–26, TLB).

PRIORITY #2 – HUSBAND

An excellent wife is the crown
of her husband (Prov. 12:4).

Solomon said, "A worthy wife is her husband's joy and crown; the other kind corrodes his strength and tears down everything he does" (Prov. 12:4, TLB). Did you catch that? A "worthy wife" versus "the other kind." He's saying that there are only two kinds of wives, and you're either one or the other. No gray area here. You're either a joy and crown, or a destroyer.

Solomon also said, "A wise woman builds her house, while a foolish woman tears hers down by her own efforts" (Prov. 14:1, TLB). Perhaps her own efforts are really a lack of effort; she gets in a rut and just stops making an effort! What have you done creatively this week to make your marriage a love affair? Not last Valentine's Day but *this week.* Let's look at the positive things a wise woman, a *creative counterpart,* does to build her relationship with the most important man in her life.

I LOVE YOU—PERIOD!

The most used word in the English language today must be *love,* but how many of us really love? We say, "I love you *if* you perform the way I want you to." Or "I love you, *and* I expect this in return." "I love you, *but* don't you get too close." "I love you *because* of the status and security you offer." *If, and, but, maybe,* or *because*—is this the way God loves us? The most exciting thing I've ever learned is that God loves me—period! He loves me unconditionally. God sent His Son to die for you and me *while* we were yet sinners —not after we had shaped our lives up! And guess what? God asks us to love our husbands as He loves us. Unconditionally, with no strings attached.

I remember when, as a new Christian in college, I first came face to face with God's love for me. I didn't know much of what was in the Bible, but I did know 1 Corinthians 13, and I read it over and over, basking in what it told me: "Love is patient, love is kind. It does not envy, it does not boast, it is not proud. It is not rude, it is not self-seeking, it is not easily angered, it keeps no record of wrongs. Love does not delight in evil but rejoices in the truth. It always protects, always trusts, always hopes, always perseveres. Love never fails" (NIV). I thought this passage was the most beautiful poetry I had ever read until one day a friend suggested I go home and read it, putting my name where the word *love* appeared, to see if this was the kind of love I had for my husband. So I started out, "Linda is patient, Linda is kind." (Gulp.) "She never envies, she does not boast, she is not proud." (Oh, no.) "Linda is not rude, she is not self-seeking, she is not easily angered." And so it went, until I was completely sobered by my responsibility to love as God loves me. Try this yourself sometime, prayerfully and with a heart receptive to God's speaking to you. This kind of love is not an option. It's a requirement.

WHO'S FIRST IN YOUR HEART?

When Joy was three, she came to me one day with a baited question, "Mommy, who do you love most, Jesus or me?" I knew she wouldn't understand if I answered "Jesus," so after some quick thinking I replied, "Honey, I love Jesus the most of the people in heaven, and I love Daddy, you, Robin, and Tommy the most of the people here on earth." She liked my answer, and she said, "Me, too! That's the way I love them, too!"

Do you show your husband that of *all* the people here on earth you love him the most? Is he sure he's first in your heart? When we moved to Philadelphia, Tommy was five weeks old, Robin eighteen months, and Joy had just turned three. Not only was I a walking zombie, but my priorities kept getting tangled. In my heart and mind Jody was first, but in my actions it never seemed to come out that way. Every time he wanted to sit and talk with me, some little person needed a diaper changed, or needed to be fed, or had some other major catastrophe! The children's needs were so immediate, so pressing. I wanted to be a good mother, but I also wanted to be a good wife. So I began to pray that God would show me at this difficult time in my life how to let Jody know he was first in my heart.

HOW ABOUT A DATE, HONEY?

The first thing God showed me was that Jody and I needed to have dates. You remember what dating is—that's what you did *before* you were married! You went out *alone* together for an entire evening! At that time Jody and I were going to a couples Bible study he taught on Tuesday evenings. So instead of getting the baby-sitter at seven-thirty, we started having her come at four-thirty or five-thirty, and we would spend two or three hours just talking.

When we had the money (which wasn't often!) we would go out to dinner. Other times we took a picnic supper, and sometimes we sat in a restaurant and had a cup of coffee. Some of our most memorable times have been spent over a cup of coffee, not spending money but communicating. I feel a couple should try to have a date every two weeks, or every week if possible. Are you moaning, "How will we ever find the time?" One thing I've learned in my twelve years of married life is that you can do anything that is important enough to you!

ALONE AT LAST

As I prayed and thought of ways to show Jody he was first in my life, the second thing I realized was that we needed *extended* time together, away from the children, a kind of second honeymoon. Being short on both money and baby-sitters, I decided to turn this one over to the Lord. I couldn't arrange it, but I knew He could. A few days later a friend, a medical doctor and the mother of five children, mentioned she had the key to a lovely apartment belonging to a fellow doctor who traveled extensively. She asked if I knew anyone in need of a place to stay. I held out my hand! By arranging to trade off with another set of parents we got baby-sitting for our children, and then we were off for a wonderful twenty-four hours together.

Two words come to mind as I reflect on our weekend retreats: *plan* and *persevere*. Once we had a three-day getaway all planned. The baby-sitter was at our house spending the night, and at 6:30 A.M. I was supposed to catch the bus to join Jody in the city where he was speaking. At 2:00 A.M. our youngest child became violently ill, and the trip had to be canceled. Shortly after that we tried again, and this time the baby-sitter got sick! ("Lord," I said, "I prayed for us and for the children but forgot the baby-sitter. Next time she'll be first on my list!") It *is* a hassle to get off alone on a date or a weekend retreat, but many of us give up too easily. Next time remember to plan and persevere!

LITTLE THINGS MEAN A LOT

When was the last time you sent a note to your husband at his job, thanking him for taking you out to dinner? Or put a note in his briefcase or lunch box telling him you love him? It only costs a few cents to send a letter, and it only takes a few minutes to write one. We write thank-you notes to *everybody*—to the neighbors who invited us over for hot dogs, to Aunt Grace who sent the lovely ceramic poodle candy dish, and to Mrs. Duzitall, who so generously gave of her time to address your ladies' club. But what about the fellow who takes you out to dinner when he'd rather collapse on the sofa, who sends you roses even though they make his nose itch, and who spends Saturday afternoons watching your offspring play soccer when the football game on television beckons him?

We somehow feel our husbands just *know* we appreciate them. Try letting him know by writing, or say it explicitly. He may not show any emotion or may even act embarassed, but inside he'll be thinking you're a pretty smart woman to have figured out what a terrific guy he is! There are hundreds of little things you can say and do to let him know you love him. Use your imagination!

CREATIVE CHRISTMAS

Before we had our children, Christmas and Jody's birthday were creative times for me. One year I saved $150 to buy him an overhead projector for Christmas. To get the money I sold blood, had our high school rings melted and sold the gold, and schemed and connived as only a woman can. I was so excited about the projector that I almost gave it to him before Christmas! The gift meant a lot to Jody, not because it was expensive but because he knew the time, effort, and love that had gone into it.

But after you have children it's such fun to buy dolls and trains, and somehow your husband doesn't seem as important anymore. Realizing this had happened to me, I began to ask God to show me something creative to give Jody for Christmas that would convey my love and appreciation for him. I knew I couldn't sell blood (after having three children in three years I didn't have much left!) and we didn't have any more rings to melt, so I figured $50 was the most I could spend. Getting him something really nice for $50 was a challenge.

It would have been easier if Jody liked clothes, but he doesn't. He likes books—so many books that we could almost open a public library in our house! That year I discovered, by some carefully veiled questioning, that his heart's secret desire was a set of scholarly commentaries selling for the low, low price of only $130! Fighting the urge to give up and just give him a tie, I called the book store to find out if the books were still in print and if I could buy them one at a time. The nice man in the store replied they were sold only as a set, but that I was in luck. They were on sale for the rock-bottom price of only $115!

I thanked him and had the receiver halfway back to the hook when he inquired, "Lady, do you *really* want those books?"

"I really do," I replied.

"Well, wait a minute," came his response. "I think another fellow who works here has a set he might want to sell."

The other fellow came to the phone and asked if I was *sure* I wanted the books. He said they were very deep, and he had given up trying to read them. I assured him my husband would *love* them!

"Well, would $50 be too much?" he asked hesitantly. "They're still in the original boxes, but I *have* made one mark in them."

I managed to stay calm while making arrangements to pick them up. Then after I hung up I literally shouted to God "with a voice of praise," thanking Him that He was concerned that my husband know he was first in my life!

GET THAT GRAY MATTER PERKING

The results of a recent survey revealed that husbands usually list a lack of variety as the main problem in their marriage. They may love their wives, but they're still just plain bored. Remember the question I asked earlier: what have you done this week to make your marriage a love affair?

I thought my busy life and three children made it hard to be creative until I was struck by the example of a friend. Nancy's husband was a resident at a local hospital, working thirty-six hours and then having twelve hours off. For this he received $400 a month. Since this wasn't enough for them to live on, he would work at other hospitals on his weekends off in order to make ends meet. The result was that they saw each other about as often as you and I see the President!

But unlike many of her friends in medical circles, Nancy refused to let this ruin their marriage. On Friday evenings when Jim couldn't come home, she would dress up their daughter and herself and would drive forty-five minutes across town in rush-hour traffic to have dinner with him in the hospital cafeteria. How many of the other wives do you think did this? Right! Jim would proudly show off his wife and little girl to all his colleagues who were munching their meat loaf and macaroni in solitude. Warmed by her demonstration of love, he would then go back to work while Nancy drove the long miles home.

And on Thanksgiving, when all the other men in America were home with their families and turkey dinners and football games on TV, Jim had to work. Undaunted, Nancy packed up the turkey and trimmings, the linen and silver, and the whole works and took it to the hospital, where she and Jim dined in elegance.

As I shared this story in a recent seminar, a woman in the audience blurted out, "How dumb!" Yes, I suppose you could look at it that way. I mean, it *was* a lot of trouble carting a hot turkey across town, and they must have looked a little strange sitting there eating in the corridor, but what do you think it communicated to Nancy's husband? As she continued to do things like this, he was assured he was more important to her than anything else, and that when he couldn't come to her, she would come to him.

And another interesting thing happened in their marriage. Nancy was a new Christian, very excited about her faith. Jim was skeptical and watched her carefully. She could have sermonized, preached, and nagged, but instead she just loved him. Before long, he too was excited about the Christian life!

PRIORITY #3 – CHILDREN
Behold, children are a gift of the Lord (Ps. 127:3, NASB).

In Isa. 28:9, 10 we read, "Whom will he teach knowledge and to whom will he explain the message? Those who are weaned from the milk, those taken from the breast. For it is precept upon precept, precept upon precept, line upon line, line upon line, here a little, there a little" (RSV). I wish I could set my three children down and in one lesson teach them all there is to know about character, godliness, manners, life and death! Wouldn't that be nice! Unfortunately, it doesn't happen quite that way. We must give them, like Isaiah says, here a little, there a little, precept upon precept, line upon line! So many times I feel nothing is going past their ears.

Then hark—I'll see some small grain of truth that has pene-
trated, encouraging me to continue giving line upon line!

LIKE MOTHER, LIKE DAUGHTER

Ecclesiastes states that what the mother is, the daughter
will turn out to be. How I groaned when I read that! The
most challenging job I have ever undertaken is being a
mother! I thought I was a patient, relatively organized person
until I had three small children. I'm convinced some of God's
greatest tools to form us into His image are our own children.

What we are speaks so much louder than what we say.
In Deuteronomy we find we must practice what we preach:
"And these words, which I am commanding you today, shall
be on your heart; and you shall teach them diligently to your
sons and shall talk of them when you sit in your house and
when you walk by the way and when you lie down and when
you rise up" (6:6–7, NASB).

Unless you have a vital relationship with God, it is impossible to impart His truth to your children as you sit in
the house, walk by the way, lie down, and rise up. These
verses depict a parent whose love and commitment to God
are so much a part of his life that he shares and relates this
wisdom and law of God to every life situation. Your children
are watching. What are they seeing in your life?

AM I REALLY THERE?

Not long ago I had a conversation with a gracious Christian
woman whose children were nearly grown. She commented,
"Linda, you teach seminars, speak, and so forth. My, you
must be out of your home a great deal of the time."

I piously replied "No, I only allow myself two mornings a
week out of my home. I'm home with my children the
majority of the time."

The dear lady sighed and said, "I could have said that,
too, when I was your age. But, you know, if I had it to do
over again, I'd do it so differently. I was in my home all right,
but I wasn't *really* there! I was on the phone planning a

luncheon, organizing the Sunday school program or a tennis tournament. And when my children came into the room, I'd shove a cookie in their hand and tell them Mommy was busy."

"Oh, Lord," I thought. "I've given a few cookies!"

God used this discussion to challenge me to evaluate my time with my children. Was I really there—available for their needs? Or was I preoccupied with other things in order to avoid the pressure and responsibility of small children? It was a sobering reflection. Even the tastiest cookie is no substitute for time and attention.

OH SUSANNA

There is a woman in history who has greatly challenged me as a mother. Her name is Susanna. She had nineteen children (a feat I feel deserves the Medal of Honor!) at a time when women nursed their babies for years. The way I figure it, this dear woman must have been either pregnant or nursing a baby her entire adult life!

She also lived at a time when there was no Colonel Sander's Kentucky Fried Chicken, no Hamburger Helper, and no Duncan Hines. Everything was made from scratch. No school was available for her children (the nine who survived into their school years), so she taught them herself! (Wouldn't that be fun?) Susanna's husband traveled, and we all know that helps life on the home front!

In a letter to her husband, Susanna related that she felt it an awesome responsibility before God to raise these children for Him. She said she had decided to spend time one evening a week with each child individually, and named the child and the night. Some nights she had to double up, since she had more than seven children. (I thought, "Oh, I'm so tired at night, how did she do it?") This woman's self-sacrifice is overwhelming! Susanna also related that on some days she was so concerned for her children, that they become the men and women God wanted, that she would spend an hour a day in prayer for them.

Was this mother's time and prayer and self-sacrifice worthwhile? Susanna's last name was Wesley. Two of her sons, John and Charles, grew up and totally transformed England by a social and spiritual revolution.

FIRST ON THE CRITICAL LIST

Psychologists say the most important thing a mother can do for her child is to love the child's father, and the most important thing a father can do for his child is to love the child's mother. A child can be loved by the mother and loved by the father, but if Mommy and Daddy don't love each other, a child can have deep feelings of insecurity.

I remember talking with Tommy when he was three. He was proudly displaying his creation from Sunday school, which said "Jesus died on the cross for my sins." I asked him what sin was, and he shrugged his shoulders. I proceeded to explain that sin is being selfish and doing naughty things. I asked him if he ever did naughty things. He said no. Marvelous! Obviously I wasn't getting through.

In an attempt to explain that sin is universal, I told him that even Mommy did things that were wrong. He said, "I know." Then he proceeded to list a few. "You 'member, Mommy, when you and Daddy was fighting? Daddy said, 'I'll cook breakfast,' and you said, 'No, I'll cook breakfast.' That was naughty to fight, wasn't it?"

I recalled the incident of two weeks before. We had not actually been fighting but kidding in loud voices. To a child, this mock fight could have been real. Of all the things I do wrong, my son zeroed in on a situation which made him feel insecure—"Mommy and Daddy was fighting."

PRIORITY #4 – HOME
She looks well to the ways of her household,
and does not eat the bread of idleness (Prov. 31:27, NASB).

We read in Proverb 31 that the excellent wife looks well

to the ways of her household and does not eat the bread of idleness. Obviously, she is a very neat and tidy housekeeper. It seems to come naturally to some people, but I'm not one of them. Recently I was visiting a friend, and as our children began to play I realized every toy her children owned was still in the box it had come in! At our house, not only do we not have the original boxes, but we also seem to lose parts of the toys!

YOU SET THE PACE

Because of the woman she is, our friend in Proverb 31 has a home that exudes a good atmosphere, making it a place people want to frequent. Every home has an atmosphere. Maybe you don't know what the atmosphere of your home is, but there are some who do—the people who frequent it. How would you describe the atmosphere in your home? Pick an adjective: warm, peaceful, loving, cheerful, united? How about anxious, bitter, contentious, or frustrated?

It is the woman in each home who creates the atmosphere. She is like the hub of the wheel around which the home revolves. Have you ever noticed how quickly your husband and children pick up your moods? When you're grumpy, your husband seems to come home grumpy, too, and your children pick up that mood the second they come in from school. Then you wonder what is the matter with them!

Try it tonight. An experiment in terror. Be a real first-class Oscar the Grouch at dinner time, and see how long it takes the others to follow suit! Better yet, be the woman God wants you to be, and see how fast they respond!

WHAT! ME ORGANIZED?

Women are sometimes criticized for taking thirty minutes to do something that should take ten. Many times the criticism is deserved. Because a woman in the home has the freedom to budget her time as she likes, often she cops out and doesn't budget at all.

Several years ago I began to make out what I call my

priority sheet, listing my priorities in a column along with my daily schedule, weekly schedule, and menu list. (See sample sheet on the next page.) Because this idea encouraged me, I have shared it with many others. It has worked for them, too. So I put together the *Priority Planner* (Thomas Nelson, 1977), a fifty-two-page booklet of double sheets with a perforated shopping list designed to help Christian women keep their priorities straight and be more efficient in the home.[2]

Sunday evening is a good planning time for me. I begin by listing one special project under each priority. Perhaps a candle-light dinner for Jody and a family slide show for the children. Next I transfer the special project under each priority to the appropriate place on the weekly schedule. Then, I fill in the major things to do for that week on the weekly schedule. Finally, I make out the daily schedule each evening. All this daily and weekly planning may seem burdensome, but planning enables you to accomplish more in less time.

Charles Schwab, one of the first presidents of Bethleham Steel Company, realized this and requested an efficiency expert, Ivy Lee, to come up with a method to pep up his employees to do the things they needed to do. Mr. Schwab said he would pay anything within reason.

Mr. Lee promised to give him something to step up his production by at least 50 percent! Handing Mr. Schwab a blank piece of paper, Ivy Lee instructed him to do the following: (1) Write down the six most important tasks you have to do tomorrow and number them in order of importance, (2) First thing tomorrow begin with item one and stick with it until you're finished, (3) After completing number one cross it out with a bright red pen! (4) Proceed to number two and complete it before going on to three.

After trying this method for a few weeks, Mr. Schwab sent Ivy Lee a check for $25,000 with a letter saying the lesson was the most profitable he had ever learned.

After only five years, this plan was credited as a major

Priorities/ _Week of_

Weekly Schedule

1 LORD • _"But seek first His kingdom and His righteousness; and all these things shall be added to you."_ **Matt. 6:33**

Memorize 3 verses

2 HUSBAND • _"An excellent wife is the crown of her husband..."_ **Prov. 12:4**

Candlelight dinner

3 CHILDREN • _"Behold, children are a gift of the Lord."_ **Psalm 127:3**

Popcorn
Slides of family

4 HOME • _"She looks well to the ways of her household, and does not eat the bread of idleness."_ **Prov. 31:27**

Paint bedroom

5 YOURSELF • _"You shall love your neighbor as yourself."_ **Matt. 19:19**

Jog
Crochet shawl

6 OUTSIDE THE HOME • _"Go therefore and make disciples of all nations..."_ **Matt. 28:19**

Bible study
Meeting

Things To Do This Week

Bring flowers to
Grandma

Take dog to vet

Monday

Begin shawl
Kids slides

Tuesday

Meeting

Wednesday

Bible study

Thursday

Friday

Candlelight dinner

Saturday

Paint bedroom

Sunday

Church

Daily Schedule

1. Get yarn – shawl
2. Grocery
3. Make fruit cocktail
4. Jog
5. Write 2 letters
6. Get slides ready

Menu

Tacos, frozen fruit cocktail

Baked fish, potatoes, salad, carrots

BBQ beef sandwiches french fries

Chicken in the Pot

Roast, potatoes, strawberry salad

Chicken-rice casserole

Spaghetti, French bread, green beans, salad

Shopping List

Taco sauce
Ground beef
Carrots
Strawberries
Chicken
French bread
Pot roast
Cereal
Detergent
Cat food

factor in turning the unknown Bethleham Steel Company into the biggest independent steel producer in the world. And it helped Charles Schwab make one hundred million dollars! [3]

Now, I won't promise you a hundred million dollars! But I am convinced you will be a more organized, happier person if you use the $25,000 plan. I have made use of the $25,000 plan by writing it in the boxes marked "Daily Schedule" in the Priority Planner.

Menus should be made out along with your priority list and weekly schedule. Plan your menus, then make out your shopping list from your menu for the week. I do this with my Priority Planner, and I tear off the shopping list Monday morning as I head out the door to the store.

Perhaps this method of planning would be helpful to you, too. If not, find one that will. The important thing is that you be faithful and do all things decently and in order. I'm convinced the reason many women are frustrated in the home is because they are not a "good boss." They don't know how to organize and use their time efficiently. They putter around getting little accomplished and then complain because they never have the time to do the things they enjoy. Wise use of the Priority Planner can change this!

A PAIN OR A CHALLENGE

Do you consider it a pain in the neck or a challenge to plan exciting meals in spite of the high prices caused by inflation? Recently I arrived home from the grocery store and began unpacking three mammoth grocery bags. Jody walked in and the barrage began. "Honey, would you believe oatmeal is now 51¢ and it used to be 33¢?" "Honey, would you believe I paid 97¢ for this box of cereal?"

After several items, I stopped and said, "I sound like the contentious woman in Proverbs, don't I?" I realized I was griping about prices and complaining to Jody when there was nothing he could do about it. He gives me as much money as he can, and it is my responsibility to create delicious, colorful, and nutritious meals with the money I have —without griping. Solomon said, "It is better to live in a corner of the roof than in a house shared with a contentious woman" (Prov. 25:24, NASB).

I read of one woman who, after concocting a meatless, high protein, good-for-you casserole of grated potatoes, carrots, onions, powdered milk and eggs, was eager for her husband's opinion. After eating a few forkfuls, he commented, "Well, it's just fine, Honey, but I wouldn't want it every year!"

Now I must put in a plug for a Crock Pot, the greatest boon to a busy wife the world has ever known! Mine has been a true blessing! As I'm writing now, my Crock Pot is at home cooking a round steak that will be completely ready for dinner tonight. It's terrific knowing that dinner is taken care of! I can cook several chicken dishes, roasts, casseroles, or just about anything in it. Usually I cook two meals at once, and freeze one. On busy days, it's a joy to pull out a meal and not have to cook!

It is an exciting challenge to learn all we can about being a homemaker. Psalm 101:2 says, "I will walk within my house with a perfect heart." Let's each take that and memorize it and ask God that our house might have this kind of woman as its mistress.

PRIORITY #5 — YOURSELF

You shall love your neighbor as yourself
(Matt. 19:19, NASB).

Everyone needs time to themselves. Time to read, to practice a hobby, or just to do nothing! As Christians we sometimes feel we must be busy every single moment. Evaluate your weekly schedule and plan into it time for yourself. You will be a better functioning wife and mother if you have some time alone each week.

TIME TO YOURSELF

If you have children, the idea of having time to yourself may sound utterly impossible. Take heart! It is possible to do anything you really want to!

I have a friend in the neighborhood with whom I trade off baby-sitting. On Monday afternoon I take care of her two children for three hours, and then Tuesday mornings she has mine for three hours. I also participate in a neighborhood baby-sitting club where several young mothers baby-sit for each other, earning "hours"—not money. Many women use a "mother's day out" program or hire a sitter. Whatever arrangements must be made, make them. You need and deserve a few hours each week to develop your creative abilities, to go shopping, or to do whatever you enjoy!

As one dear woman in her fifties put it, "My husband finds me a much more interesting person when I have interests and activities that broaden me and develop me as a person." God wants to develop you as a woman. Give him some working time!

PRIORITY #6 – OUTSIDE THE HOME

Go therefore and make disciples of all nations
(Matt. 28:19, NASB).

I was sharing my excitement about the priorities of a woman's life with a group of women in upstate New York, and one woman said "Linda, I cannot believe what you are saying. I know that you believe the Great Commission to go into the world and preach the gospel was given to women as well as to men, yet here you are saying that our service for Christ is at the end of the list! Since becoming a Christian two years ago, my service for the Lord has been first!" I smiled and told her I'd like to ask her husband how he liked that!

When my three children were very young, I decided before God to keep my priorities in the order I've just shared. I constantly re-evaluate where I spend my time and seek to keep God first, Jody second, the children third, my home fourth, me fifth, and my outside activities sixth. Many times this is very difficult. It is *easier* to teach a Bible study than to stay home with three sick children. I fail many times, but I always come back to those same priorities. It's hard to describe the joy and satisfaction of knowing you are where God wants you and you are doing exactly what He wishes you to do. When you go along with God, amazing things result!

SATISFACTION GUARANTEED

When we moved to Philadelphia, I asked God to use me in the lives of women—to teach, to train, to share the good news of eternal life in Jesus Christ. I had no idea how God would accomplish that prayer! I had no car, I had one friend, and I had three little children. Not the most perfect combination to reach out to others! However, through my friend I met two other women, shared with them how to have evangelistic coffees, and began Bible study groups. As I began this project, I decided to be out of my home one to two mornings a week.

Throughout the year I kept my commitment, and I was overwhelmed by what God accomplished. Five Bible study groups were started, several women were trained, and many accepted Christ as their personal Savior. More was accomplished in that one year when I was out two mornings a week than when I spent *all* my time ministering to women before I had children! God blessed my ministry, because I was where He wanted me. My outreach was multiplied when I kept my priorities in order.

Once while we were in upstate New York, it snowed furiously. Jody was at a conference with the car while I was home pregnant with our third child. I remember thinking, "Lord, I would love to talk to someone older than two." Then I remembered Jody had driven to the conference with another man, and I decided to call the man's wife. I didn't know her, but I figured she may be lonely, too.

As we talked, I realized she didn't understand why her husband had left her alone and gone with Jody. She was confused about his new commitment to Christ. When I found out she had a car, I invited her and her son to dinner and to spend the night. As we sat in our living room that night, I had the privilege of sharing the good news of Jesus Christ and seeing her commit her life to Him. God again showed me He can use me right where I am as I keep my priorities in order.

VARIETY IS THE SPICE OF LIFE

Each of us is at a different time in life; each has varying responsibilities. Some of us have energy overflowing, and some are sagging by four in the afternoon. As one friend put it, "Some women can run three-ring circuses, some two-ring, and some one-ring." It isn't important how many rings you have. What is important is that before God you know yourself, your talents, and your emotional spiritual, and physical capacities. "For I say, through the grace given unto me, to every man that is among you, not to think of himself more highly than he ought to think; but to think soberly, according as God had dealt to every man the measure of faith" (Rom. 12:3, KJV). You do not need to do everything your neighbor does. You are not your neighbor; you are you!

I know at this time in my life just how much I can handle outside my home and still be the wife and mother I want to be. In a few years, I will be able to do more. Each of us needs to honestly evaluate and plan with our own capacities in mind.

WORKING WIVES

I can just hear some of you who work at an outside job saying, "All of this is fine and good for you homemakers, but it won't work for me!" Yes it will! If you work, your work is priority number six. You will not be able to spend the same quantity of time with your husband, children, or on your home, but the quality of time can be just the same. If you work, you should be even more organized than the home-maker—dinners made on the weekends, up early to get every-thing in order, etc. You can still plan candlelight dinners for your husband and do many of the things I've shared. I find women in the home use their children as an excuse for their lack of creativity, and women who work use their work as an excuse. With each it takes much creativity, hard work, and perseverance, but it is worth it! Your attitude is the key: do your husband and children feel they are most important, or do they feel you are "in love" with your work? I'm not saying it's easy—I'm saying it is well worth the effort!

PITFALLS

As we talk about our priorities, I must warn about four problem areas.

1. We forget priority number 1. *Activity* for God is sub-stituted for a *relationship* with Him.
2. We put the children before our husband. Consciously or unconsciously in word or in deed, we put the chil-dren's wants and needs before our husband's.
3. We put our outside activities before one or all!
4. We fail to realize that as the years pass the emphasis we put in different priority areas will change. We need to constantly re-evaluate our priority list.

A LIFE THAT COUNTS

I have a friend who is a missionary with her husband and children in Latin America. On a vacation, she was bitten by a scorpion and lay near death for two days. When she knew she would live, she wrote down some of the thoughts she had had as she lay dying. "If it ends now for me, I wish it would have counted for more."

But immediately I thought, "That is so foolish. It has

counted with my husband and children where God has given me the most, along with the most responsibility." That is not to say my life was perfect or couldn't have been more, but it seemed God was saying to me, "Do not be a child, thinking those thoughts. You have counted where I have put you!"

MY OWN ROBERT REDFORD

Chapter Five

One woman, when asked the difference between infatuation and love, answered: "Infatuation is when you think that he's as sexy as Robert Redford, as smart as Henry Kissinger, as noble as Ralph Nader, as funny as Woody Allen, and as athletic as Jimmy Conners. Love is when you realize that he's as sexy as Woody Allen, as smart as Jimmy Conners, as funny as Ralph Nader, as athletic as Henry Kissinger, and nothing like Robert Redford—but you'll take him anyway!" [1]

Acceptance is taking him just as he is—strengths and weaknesses. Let's look together at God's view of partner acceptance and what He has said about it. There are two commands given to wives, both found in Ephesians 5. The first is to reverence your husband and the second is to be submissive to him. We'll take the easiest first and start with reverence!

The Greek word for *reverence* means "to be afraid of" or "fear," to be in awe of someone or to respect deeply. We see Sarah calling Abraham "Lord." What does this mean to us today? Are you to call your husband "Lord," say "yes, sir" and bow or curtsy to him? Perhaps some husbands wouldn't think that was such a bad idea!

In the Amplified Bible, Eph. 5:33 is translated, "And let the wife see that she respects and reverences her husband—that she notices him, regards him, honors him, prefers him, venerates and esteems him, and that she defers to him, praises him, and loves and admires him exceedingly!"

This passage makes it clear we are to reverence our husbands, but many of us feel it is our God-ordained responsibility to revamp them! We feel that getting a husband is like buying an old house. We don't see it the way it is, but the way it's going to be when we get it remodeled!

Reverence is positive—it's an active verb. When you reverence, you do something to show your admiration and respect. Perhaps the thought of admiring and honoring your husband is foreign to you, maybe even repulsive.

Many of us are so wrapped up in the negative aspects of our husbands that we ignore the positive. A woman who will not accept her husband as he is cannot reverence him. Before we can talk about reverencing, admiring, and uplifting our husbands, we must learn to accept them as they are—no strings attached.

In the early years of our marriage, Jody called me his "personal Holy Spirit." Wasn't he fortunate! I was sent by God to convict him of sin, judgment, and righteousness. I was sent to instruct him in proper etiquette, apparel, and personal habits, and it didn't work.

All of us are human, and we all have faults. When we live with someone day after day, it is easy to become irritated with his or her faults, and even become obsessed with them. When asked to distinguish *love* from *like,* one man answered, "*Love* is the same as *like* except you feel sexier and more romantic. And also more annoyed when he talks with his mouth full. And you resent it more when he interrupts you. And you also respect him less when he shows any weakness."

Many areas in my own life need changing, and many areas in my husband's life need work. I'm sure the same is true for you and your husband as well! How do we change? How do we cause our husbands to change? Of course you can try being a "personal Holy Spirit." You can try nagging, belittling, suggesting, advising until you faint from exhaustion. This is usually the human way of pursuing change.

OUR WAY OF EFFECTING CHANGE

It's easy to talk yourself into trying to change your husband instead of allowing God His way. Why do we want our husbands to change?

MOTIVATIONS FOR CHANGE

1. *Because his habits irritate us.* Saturday morning rolls around and you're up at seven, sleepily pouring cereal into the bowls and realizing that Saturday is no different from any other day. How you'd like to sleep (especially when Happy Harry is snoring away)! As the clock reaches nine, then ten, your irritation grows. You slam doors, find reasons to go into the bedroom, and make snide remarks about hoping lover boy is enjoying his rest, and go into the other room and fume.

One husband's irritating habit was his erratic bath time! "At one time I was uptight about the time of day my husband took his bath! He got up, dressed, ate breakfast, read the paper, and then undressed and bathed. Imagine wasting all that time by dressing twice! I suggested, reasoned, nagged, pleaded and ridiculed until we both felt our marriage balanced precariously on his bath time! Months passed before I realized that he had to get up earlier to compensate for wasted time. He worked hard enough to earn the right to 'waste time' however he wanted. Futhermore, he heads this house; therefore he has freedom to bathe any hour of the day or night he chooses. (I still think it's silly, but I keep my opinion to myself. At 42, he should be old enough to know when to bathe.)" [2]

2. *Because of a self-righteous attitude.* Doris was so holy she went to church every time the door was open. Each time, she reminded Larry that he should go; he needed to go. And every time she said it he decided again to stay home.

3. *For his benefit.* Sherry deeply loved her husband, all 250 pounds of him! His weight problem bothered her be-

cause she was certain he would have a heart attack at age forty or become a diabetic if he didn't get that weight off! She was constantly nagging Chuck to lose weight, and tried everything to make him do it. The more she nagged, the more he ate. She would prepare low-calorie meals, and he would eat on the side. Her desire for him to change stemmed from a sincere motive, but it still didn't work!

4. *What will people think?* You really do love your husband and you're convinced if he would dress in some of the "in" styles, instead of that old double-breasted jacket he wears so often, he would be more highly thought of by others.

Every wife wants her husband to be liked and accepted by her family, and I was no exception! My family lives on the beach in Southern California, and to them, heaven is spending an entire day lying on the sand doing nothing. My dear husband does not know how to "do nothing." On our trips to California, he always took his books so that while the family was basking in the sun, sand, and surf, Jody was in the house reading Athanasius' *Exposition of the Hypostatic Union.* I was sure my family would think that very odd, so I went to work being "personal Holy Spirit"!

"Honey, don't you like the sun? It really is nice" . . . ad nauseum. Jody continued to read, and I continued to suspect that my family was convinced I'd married a weirdo. (Of course, they felt no such thing.)

God finally succeeded in getting me to accept Jody just as he is, a wonderful individual created by God for a special purpose. When I allowed Jody the freedom to be what he is, a scholar, he reciprocated by trying to be all I desired.

Not long after one of our California visits, he returned for a speaking engagement and visited my family. He wrote me from their home. "Dear Honey. Would you believe in one day I have gone on a boat ride, laid in the sun, ridden a bike, walked to the fun zone, and gone swimming? I am the well-rounded all-American boy!"

5. *For the sake of the children.* Your heart-felt motivation

behind wanting your husband to have nice table manners is to set an example for the children. Is that so wrong? What about the church elder who swears at home in front of the children, and they see what a hypocrite he is. Shouldn't a wife see that he changes his ways?

We've looked at some of our motivations for forcing our husbands to change. Now let's look at some of the areas in their lives we try to change.

AREAS FOR CHANGE[3]

1. *His personal habits.* Perhaps it's the way he hangs up his towel (in a pile on the bathroom floor), or maybe his violent temper tantrums.

Paula's husband had a drinking problem. As the drinking increased, so did his time away from home. Night after night he would come in early in the morning smelling of liquor and the perfume of other women. Paula threatened, screamed, and cried, but to no avail.

When she became a Christian, she began to ask God to enable her to love her husband just as he was. I'm sure you'll agree this was no small task! Paula quit belittling her husband before the children. When they asked where he was, she simply said that he was with his friends. When she heard him stumble in at three in the morning, she got up and told him she had prepared his favorite dinner and would like to get it for him.

The poor man was stupefied. Paula continued to give, and by Christmas her husband said with tears in his eyes, "I wish I could give you a sober husband by Christmas, but I can't."

It would be a nice fairy tale if I told you that one week later he changed. It wasn't one week. More like one year, during which time Paula continued to suffer. Recently Paula communicated to a friend that the changes in their home were remarkable. She said her husband had stopped drinking, had accepted Christ as his Savior, and the family was happier than they had ever been.

2. *His attitude toward the children.* Many women would like to see their husbands spend more time with the children. Others would like their husband to set up regular devotional times with the children. A few would just like their husbands to be home long enough to confirm the rumor that the children do actually have a father!

3. *His handling of the finances.* Wives long for their husbands to be financially responsible. I have known women who have hidden money from their husbands, hidden checkbooks, and kept secret bank accounts. Others have doled out allowances to their husbands like they were little boys. When a husband is irresponsible with money, his wife becomes increasingly insecure, and insecurity is crippling to a marriage.

4. *Sex life.* One woman put the problem very well when she said, "I'm tired of Harry's Neanderthal approach to sex. After the 10 o'clock news he says in a monotone, 'You wanna do it?' "

5. *His lack of spiritual leadership.* In the early years of our marriage, we belonged to a wonderful church. Because I was Jody's "personal Holy Spirit," it was important to me that he be well thought of. Jody doesn't like to sing, and during church he would stand like a toy soldier staring off into space while everyone was singing. I was afraid people would think he was disinterested because of his lack of involvement.

So I swooped into action, nudging him, whispering in his ear that he should sing, and later giving him a lengthy discourse on the merits of singing in church. Of course this didn't change Jody. It only resulted in a quarrel on the way home. It embarasses me that I nagged and quarreled about such a relatively insignificant thing, but it seems many of us wives choose to argue over the insignificant. Nagging will not produce a spiritual giant. Only God the Holy Spirit can do that!

6. *His social habits.* I have a friend, Joan, who is from a wealthy family in St. Louis. While a student, Joan fell in love with a West Texas farmboy. (He wasn't really a hick, but then not exactly what you'd find in high society either!) As happens with engaged couples, Joan and Steve went to St. Louis for a party given by her relatives. Everyone wanted to meet her fiancé!

The meal was lovely, with roast beef, potatoes, and delicious gravy. Steve had a piece of roll and some gravy left, so he did what every self-respecting West Texan would do: sopped up the gravy with his bread! Watching in horror, Joan surreptitiously took her salad fork and jabbed it into his leg under the table. Steve was furious and didn't say another word during the dinner. Joan said her relatives thought he had little personality because he was so quiet. But she knew!

7. *His aspirations, or lack of them.* Some husbands work themselves into a heart attack. Others seem to have no ambition whatever. One wife told me she knew her hubsand could become president of the company but that he had no desire to do it. He was perfectly content where he was. She had other plans for him, however, and the inevitable quarrels resulted.

8. *His household duties.* The garbage, the light bulbs, the outdoor Christmas tree lights! At our house, the Christmas tree lights came down on March 17! I was beginning to think it might be good to just leave them up until next year! Plenty of wives have gripes about male procrastination where duties are concerned.

9. *His time with you.* Perhaps you feel slighted because your husband spends so much time at his office or on the golf course or with the "boys." One wife tried nagging, crying, screaming, and everything she could think of to make her

husband see that she needed him home before 10:00 P.M. Finally, she decided to change her tactics. She began to do things like taking dinner to his office and writing him love notes. He began staying home more—and liking it!

RESULTS

We've seen some of the motivations and rationalizations behind wanting our husbands to change. We've seen some of the areas in their lives we try to change. What are the results of trying to revamp a husband *your* way?

1. *Tension.* Even when you truly love each other, the fierce competition of wills causes marital tension, which invariably erupts in disastrous ways.

2. *Destruction of love.* When you try to change a man, you pit yourself against him. Many men have stopped loving a wife who consistently acts like a combination mother, spiritual advisor, and dietician.

3. *Rebellion.* Most men like to come up with the ideas. If you nag him to diet, for instance, very likely he will rebel. He knows he needs to diet but will fight your attempt to run his life.

4. *Discouragement.* A man wants his wife to be proud of him. By your nagging and trying to change him, you are saying, "I really don't like you as you are."

5. *Hindering God's work.* It's our job to make our husbands whole; it's God's responsibility to make them holy. Isn't that fantastic! God gave wives to husbands to love them, to build them up, and to make them happy. God the Holy Spirit does not need us to be "personal Holy Spirits." He will work alone to bring about the needed changes in their lives. God has a special and unique plan for you and your marriage. His timing may not be your timing, but you can be assured He is at work!

So, man's way of getting change doesn't work. God, on the other hand, guarantees results!

What is God's way?

GOD'S WAY OF EFFECTING CHANGE

Step 1. *Total acceptance.*

If you want to win the deep love of your husband, you must accept him as he is with no condition of change. You must be satisfied with this total person as he exists now. You prove your contentment with an acceptance of him by not trying to change him.

I can hear you saying, "That is humanly impossible!"

You're right!

The basis of partner acceptance is the cross of Jesus Christ. Until we have been totally forgiven, we cannot forgive. *Until we have been totally loved and accepted ourselves, we cannot love and accept our husbands.*

I'd like to share with you how God brought me to a point where I was able to begin to forgive, love unconditionally, and accept my husband and others just as they are—with no condition of change.

As a young girl I was religious, and I was labeled the "all-American girl." I tried hard and usually attained whatever I aimed for in life. I figured that at the end of my life God would weigh my good works against my bad, and if the good works tipped the scale, I'd be in! Then, as a teen-ager I came up against a problem for which I had no solution. My father was an alcoholic, and during my growing up years, I had grown to resent him. He had torn our family apart, had terribly hurt my mother, brother, and me, and I found it very difficult to forgive and accept him.

Although my wonderful mother provided stability in the midst of suffering, I had insecurities, and they manifested themselves in my relationships with boys. From junior high school on, I always had someone! A class ring, a fraternity pin, a commitment to marry, and yet the relationships never lasted. I was the fickle of the fickle! Deep down I was afraid that when I married, I would be happy for six months, and then find someone that looked better! This had been the pattern for so many years, I questioned whether I could love with a lasting and committed love.

As a college student I was invited to hear a speaker talk about the claims of Jesus Christ. I went because I was religious, and besides, I was interested in the boy who had invited me. That night I heard for the first time that Christianity is not a list of rules, it is not an ethical code of a philosophy of life. It is a relationship. A relationship with Jesus Christ. And I learned that I could enter into this relationship by realizing that I needed Christ, that I could not earn my way to heaven by my good life, by my sincere efforts, or by my religious activity.

Never had I been willing to admit that I was sinful. Sin was murder and adultery, and besides, I tried hard! Sincerity had to count for something!

Through God's word I realized that sin is not just "deeds" but attitudes—an attitude of indifference or independence of God—and that my sins or selfishness was what separated me from God. Christ was the only one who could forgive my sin.

A story put it into focus for me. Suppose while driving down a street a woman named Gail received a speeding ticket and was summoned to appear in court. As she stood before the judge, she was declared guilty, and the sentence was fifty dollars or five days. Meekly she began to open her checkbook, but just then the judge stood up and took off his robe. Gail saw to her astonishment it was her father! He came toward her and said, "Gail, you're guilty. You've transgressed the law, and you deserve to pay the penalty. But because I love you, I want to pay it for you." With that, he pulled out his checkbook and wrote a check for fifty dollars.

This is a picture of exactly what God, our Father, did when

Jesus died on the cross. God, the righteous judge, declared us guilty of sin, but as our loving Father He did not want us to have to pay the penalty of eternal death and separation from Him. So God sent His only Son to die that you and I might be forgiven and have eternal life. When Jesus Christ screamed his final words from the cross, "It is finished," or literally from the Greek, "Paid in full," He was paying my penalty and yours just as the judge in the story.

The penalty had been paid, but Gail still had to make a decision. Would she be a rebellious child and defiantly say, "Thanks but no thanks. You can keep your check. I'll do it myself"? Or would she reach out and gratefully accept the gift offered in love? This story helped me slowly realize that I personally needed to reach out and accept God's gift.

For twenty years I had been trying to grow and yet had not been born spiritually. One day I quietly locked the door and pulled down the shades (God forbid that anyone should see me!) and told God I was a fake—I'd gone through all the religious motions and called myself a Christian, never knowing who Jesus Christ really is and what He has done for me. Very simply I prayed, telling God of my need, thanking Him for sending Christ to die for me on the cross, and asking Christ to come into my life, forgive my sins, and make me into the kind of woman He wanted me to be. I knew I had been totally forgiven by God and that I was totally loved and accepted by Him.

As I continued to grow in His love, I was able to go to my father and forgive him and love him just as he was. I also knew I was now able to make a commitment to love someone else as God had loved me, unconditionally with no strings attached. If you have never received Christ as your Savior and Lord, you can change your eternal destiny now by quietly putting down this book and inviting Christ to come into your life and forgive your sins.

God's grace is the foundation of partner acceptance. I personally believe it is very difficult, if not impossible, to accept your husband unless you have experienced God's forgiveness and acceptance yourself. Now that you understand step 1, God's love and acceptance, you're ready to go on to step 2, applying this concept to your husband.

Step 2. *Get rid of the log in your own eye.*

Why do you see the speck that is in your brother's eye, but do not notice the log that is in your own eye? Or how can you say to your brother, 'Let me take the speck out of your eye,' when there is the log in your own eye? You hypocrite, first take the log out of your own eye, and then you will see clearly to take the speck out of your brother's eye (Matt. 7:3–5, RSV).

Often we are so concerned with our husband's faults we cannot see our own! Jay Adams begins his marriage counseling with the following project (see sample next page). In the left-hand column list all your mate's faults. Then in the right-hand column list seventy-five of your wrong responses to those faults. Perhaps your husband's fault is that he is messy. What is your response? Do you nag, sigh, scream, give him the silent treatment, or perhaps you throw the clothes he leaves lying around?

I encourage you to do this exercise. Do it now. Get out a piece of paper and make your columns. List your husband's faults and as many of your wrong responses as you can think of. You'll be surprised that your responses are as bad or worse than the faults. After you have finished, confess your wrong attitudes to God and burn the paper. Definitely *do not* show it to your husband. This exercise is for *your* benefit—to help you get the log out of your own eye!

STEP 2 – LOG REMOVAL

FAULTS	WRONG RESPONSES
1. Lack of time spent with children	1. Nag
	2. Belittle
	3. Sigh and moan
	4. Compare with other men
	5. Criticize
	6. Neglect
	7. Reject as person
	8. Cool sexually
	9. Anger
	10. Indifference
	11. Gossip to other women
	12. Publically tear him down
	13. Quote Bible verses
	14. Feel self-righteous
	15. Feel bitter
	16. Silence

Step 3. *Give your rights to God.*

We often feel that because we have tried hard or because of our sense of justice, we *deserve* to have a husband who performs properly in all areas! So we want our husbands to change to meet our expectations. This attitude is a key barrier to accepting him at face value. In order to get rid of your expectations, you must lay aside what you feel you *deserve* in a husband.

"Do nothing from selfishness or empty conceit" (Phil. 2:3,

NASB). Many times the desire to change your husband springs from selfish motives—the underlying motive being your personal benefit. Our real focus is on ourselves. Jesus says, "in humility we are to count others better than ourselves," and "others" includes husbands! "Have this attitude ... which was also in Christ Jesus, who, although he existed in the form of God, did not regard equality with God a thing to be grasped" (Phil. 2:5–6, NASB). Christ was God and deserved all of the rights of Deity. He did not regard equality with God a thing to be grasped. He didn't consider his rights as an equal with God something He should cling to. If Jesus didn't cling to his "rights" as Deity, then we should follow his example. Lay aside what you think you *deserve* in a husband and give up your expectations of change. Look at what Christ did: He "emptied Himself, taking the form of a bond-servant, and being made in the likeness of men" (Phil. 2:7, NASB). He emptied himself, laying aside the rights of Deity. His focus became serving others rather than serving himself. Too often our focus is desiring that our husbands change to suit us—not for their own benefit but for ours.

What was Christ's reward? Was it praise from men? No. It was praise from God!

"Therefore God has highly exalted him and bestowed on him the name which is above every name" (Phil. 2:9).

Because Christ laid aside all his rights to do God's will and adopted a servant's heart, God has highly exalted him! His reward was from God. One woman protested, "I tried this before for two weeks. I gave up all my rights and my husband still didn't change." The reward she wanted was a changed husband. The reward she should have been seeking was praise from God. We do this not because of what we are going to get but because we are being a faithful servant.

Wouldn't you like another exercise? On the next page there is a list of the nine areas you might like to see changed in your husband. On a sheet of paper, copy this chart and fill in what you have wanted changed in each area. Add others if you like! Now write Phil. 2:5–7 over the chart and throw it away. Now that you have given up your rights to everything you feel you "deserve" in a husband, you will be free to emphasize the positive.

CATEGORY OF EXPECTATION	DESIRED CHANGE (My "Rights")
1. Personal Habits	A neat, tidy husband who *always* hangs towels and clothes and puts away shoes!
2. Children	A husband who takes a deep interest in everything the children do, disciplines, instructs, and plays with the children!
3. Finances	A husband who is financially responsible, pays bills on time, and gives me *lots* of extra money!
4. Sex	A husband who is *very* romantic, tender, exciting, sensitive, and loving!
5. Spiritual	
6. Social	

7. Aspirations

8. Duties

9. Time

Step 4. *Discern positive qualities.*
"Finally brethren, whatever is true, whatever is honorable, whatever is just, whatever is pure, whatever is lovely, whatever is gracious, if there is any excellence, if there is anything worthy of praise, think about these things" (Phil. 4:8, RSV).

Does your husband get up and go to work? Thank God for this. Does he want to be a man of God? Thank God for this. Does he play with the children? Thank God for this.

In fact, why don't you thank God for everything positive about him. Take out another sheet of paper and write down *all* the things you have to be thankful for about your husband. You don't need to tear this one up; in fact, you can show it to him!

Step 5. *Ask your husband's forgiveness.*
"So if you are standing before the altar in the Temple, offering a sacrifice to God, and suddenly remember that a friend has something against you, leave your sacrifice there beside the altar and go and apologize and be reconciled to him, and then come and offer your sacrifice to God" (Matt. 5:23–24, TLB).

Some of us have totally alienated our husbands through our failure to accept them. We have wounded their male egos deeply and have caused them to rebel against us. Each situation is different, and many of you do not need to ask your husband's forgiveness, but some of you do. Before you can begin building your marriage, before you can reverence and submit to your husband, you need to seek his forgiveness for your wrong attitudes. Do not do this hastily as an emotional gesture because of reading this book. Think about it, pray about it, and ask God's wisdom concerning whether you should ask his forgiveness, and if so, how you should ask it.

If after much prayer and thought you feel the need to clean the slate and admit your wrong to him, approach him in such a way that *all the blame is cast on you.* For instance, do not say "Honey, because you've been such a hard person to live with and because of your many bad habits, I have not been a good wife." Remember, you are asking forgiveness, not telling him his faults!

Perhaps you could say something like this: "Honey, I've recently realized that I have not loved you as I should, and I want to ask your forgiveness." or "Honey, I know that I have not been considerate of your feelings, and I want to ask you to forgive me." Then ask him, "Will you forgive me?"

As I said, many of you will feel no need to ask forgiveness. You can go right on to the positive. But for others, the dirt must be removed from the glass before it can be filled with clean, fresh water.

Step 6. *Verbalize your acceptance.*

And that is what the next chapter is about! Reverence is putting your total acceptance into practice. Once you accept your husband as he is with no condition of change, you are ready to begin to notice him, regard him, honor him, prefer him, venerate and esteem him, praise and love and admire him exceedingly!

HIS GREATEST FAN

Chapter Six

He began his life with all the classic handicaps and disadvantages. His mother was a powerfully built, domineering woman who found it difficult to love anyone. She had been married three times, and her second husband divorced her because she beat him up regularly. The father of the child I'm describing was her third husband; he died of a heart attack a few months before the child's birth. As a consequence, the mother had to work long hours from his earliest childhood. She gave him no affection, no love, no discipline, and no training during those early years. She even forbade him to call her at work. Other children had little to do with him, so he was alone most of the time. He was absolutely rejected from his earliest childhood. He was ugly and poor and untrained and unlovable. When he was thirteen years old a school psychologist commented that he probably didn't even know the meaning of the word "love." During adolescence, the girls would have nothing to do with him and he fought with the boys. Despite a high IQ, he failed academically, and finally dropped out during his third year of high school. He thought he might find a new acceptance in the Marine Corps; they reportedly built men, and he wanted to be one. But his problems went with him. The other Marines laughed at him and ridiculed him. He fought back, resisted authority, and was court-martialed and thrown out of the marines with an undesirable discharge. So there he was

—a young man in his early twenties—absolutely friend-
less and shipwrecked. He was small and scrawny in
stature. He had an adolescent squeak in his voice. He
was balding. He had no talent, no skill, no sense of
worthiness. He didn't even have a driver's license. Once
again he thought he could run from his problems so he
went to live in a foreign country. But he was rejected
there too. Nothing had changed. While there, he married
a girl who herself had been an illegitimate child and
brought her back to America with him. Soon, she began
to develop the same contempt for him that everyone
else displayed. She bore him two children, but he never
enjoyed the status and respect that a father should have.
His marriage continued to crumble. His wife demanded
more and more things that he could not provide. Instead of being his ally against the bitter world, as he
hoped, she became his most vicious opponent. She
could outfight him, and she learned to bully him. On
one occasion, she locked him in the bathroom as
punishment. Finally, she forced him to leave. He tried
to make it on his own but he was terribly lonely. After
days of solitude, he went home and literally begged her
to take him back. He surrendered all pride. He crawled.
He accepted humiliation. He came on her terms. Despite
his meager salary, he brought her seventy-eight dollars
as a gift, asking her to take it and spend it any way she
wished. But she laughed at him. She belittled his feeble
attempts to supply the family's needs. She ridiculed his
failure. She made fun of his sexual impotency in front
of a friend who was there. At one point, he fell on his
knees and wept bitterly, as the greater darkness of his
private nightmare enveloped him. Finally in silence, he
pleaded no more. No one wanted him. No one had ever
wanted him. He was perhaps the most rejected man of
our time. His ego lay shattered in fragmented dust. The
next day, he was a strangely different man. He arose,
went to the garage and took down a rifle he had hidden

there. He carried it with him to his newly acquired job at a book-storage building. And from a window on the third floor of that building, shortly after noon, Nov. 22, 1963, he sent two shells crashing into the head of President John Kennedy. Lee Harvey Oswald, the rejected, unlovable failure, killed the man who, more than any other man on earth, embodied all the success, beauty, wealth and family affection which he lacked. In firing that rifle, he utilized the one skill he had learned in his entire, miserable lifetime.[1]

When I first read this about Lee Harvey Oswald in the excellent book *Hide or Seek* by James Dobson, I was overwhelmed by one thought: Would the story have been different if his wife had been his ally against the cruel world instead of his most bitter opponent? Could he have slowly but surely grown into a mature man if his wife had stood behind him, been on his team and admired him?

Psychiatrists say a man's most basic needs, apart from warm sexual love, are approval and admiration. In our society there is an epidemic of inferiority. Many times marriage problems are essentially personal problems, and often the personal problems are related to a bad "self-image." Many of the problems in our society are due to the fact that men will not be men. They will not assume leadership. The reason they refuse to take the lead is often due to deep-seated fears and insecurities. Because this occurs at an emotional level, it is often difficult to express.

The word *reverence* means "to stand in awe of," which encompasses "to respect, honor, esteem, adore, praise, enjoy and admire." Admiration is one major thing a wife can do to build up her husband's self-image. Even if your husband already has a healthy view of himself, *God can use your admiration to build him into more of the man God wants him to be* and into the husband you want him to be!

Your husband's self-image is directly connected to your private and public admiration and praise. It has been said,

"Behind every great man there is a great woman." I feel a great woman is one who would admire, build up, and glorify her husband, thus transforming and enhancing his image of himself. There are three key words to building your husband's self-image. 1. *Accept* him at face value. 2. *Admire* his manly qualities. 3. Submit to his *authority*.

YOUR PRIVATE LIFE

Do you build up or destroy? What do you communicate to your husband when he walks in the door after work? Genuine encouragement, or dissatisfaction? Does your face light up when he talks to you or does he see sneers and a lack of trust? A man can have everything outside the home, but if the sincere respect of his wife and children is missing he can be totally emasculated.

George was such a man. Anyone who knew him would laugh if you suggested *he* could ever be emasculated! George had everything. He had always excelled; he had always been the best at everything he tried. After graduating from law school, he easily acquired a $100,000-a-year job. He was highly respected by his peers, his employers, and by everyone in the business community. With athletic prowess, wealth, and success, what more could any man want?

The *more* George desperately wanted and needed was the respect and admiration of his wife. Instead of being his *counterpart,* she had set herself up to win the victory in their home. If he excelled, she would excel more. They each did their "own thing," but she was determined *her* "own thing" would be better than *his!* Gradually her attitude began to destroy him emotionally. Distracted and unhappy, he lost his job.

In desperation, he agreed to work with her writing a book on modern marriage. The book sold more than 200,000 copies propagating the "do your own thing" philosophy, yet their own marriage was in pathetic shape. His wife left him, and he went to work as a janitor.

Then a friend of ours met and shared the love of Jesus

Christ with him. He responded and accepted Christ, and his life began to change. He saw for the first time what happened in his marriage and why. He saw the roles God had given husbands and wives, and he realized his marriage had been a blasphemy.

George wrote a letter to his wife, asking her forgiveness for his failure to be the head of their home. He told her of his desire to have a renewed marriage in Chirst. His marriage is not together yet, but with the encouragement of Christ, he has put his own life together. He has acquired another lucrative job in the legal profession, making use of his capabilities, and is on the road to being the man God wants him to be.

I hear you saying, "That is a pretty far-out example! From an executive to a janitor, all because of a woman!" Sure, it's far out. Even though it doesn't always happen to this extreme when a wife fails to give her husband the reverence that God intended and that he desperately needs, tragic things can and will happen.

IN THE PUBLIC EYE

Just what are they seeing? What image of your husband do others receive from you? God says you should be publishing his virtues, broadcasting your love and admiration for him by all you do and say. Do your neighbors and friends think your husband is wonderful or a slob? Where did they get their information?

In Proverb 31 we read that "her husband was known in the gates when he sits among the elders of the land." One modern writer interpreted this: "Her husband is highly thought of by others because she never berates him."

A national sales executive came to New York City and put an ad in the paper with an offer to twenty men who would meet his qualifications. He offered $35,000 a year for five years plus $250,000 to a million dollars to start their own businesses. He opened shop in a motel room for three weeks, interviewing men for eighteen hours a day. At the end of three weeks he had his twenty men.

He then did a very unusual thing. He asked to interview the wives of the twenty men. One by one the women came, and after talking with all twenty women, he had only nine men left. He said he did not interview the women to determine their intelligence, their beauty, or their poise. He interviewed each woman to see if she was on her husband's team and would stand behind him. He said he was offering the men a great opportunity, but one which would require hard work and dedication. He knew that without the encouragement and praise of their wives the men would not succeed. Would your husband have been one of the nine men left?

It seems clear from Ephesians 5 that a wife is to admire her husband and build him up. Most of us know from experience that every man, woman, and child needs admiration. So why do many of us fail to give our men the admiration they need?

BARRIERS TO ADMIRATION

Feeling of awkwardness. Isn't it strange that we can admire a friend's hairdo, hanging plants, or Hungarian goulash but often cannot or will not express admiration to our husbands. Maybe we're afraid it will embarrass them or make them feel awkward. Some people just don't know how to accept compliments.

My husband is too self-centered already. I have heard women express this many times as a reason for their lack of admiration. Perhaps his egotism or boasting is a cry for admiration. No one else builds him up, so he has to.

No apparent admirable qualities. In 1 Corinthians 13, we read that love "believes all things." One woman, when told to express admiration toward her husband, said that there was simply nothing about him to admire. The teacher asked her to go far back into their marriage and find something she had admired. Obediently the woman went home and told her husband she had admired the way he handled their money during the Depression. (I call that really delving back!) The poor man, starved for admiration and appreciation, turned to his wife with tears in his eyes. He had been longing for that for over thirty years!

Goethe, the German author, said that if you treat a man as he is, he will stay as he is, but if you treat him as if he were what he ought to be, and could be, he will become the bigger and better man.

Jesus was a master at seeing people—not as they were, but as they could be. The apostle Peter is a perfect example. Peter the impulsive, Peter the anxious (he reminds me of me), always ready to leap before looking. Jesus said to this impulsive fisherman, "Cephas, you shall be Peter," meaning "the Rock." Now Peter was a lot of things, but one thing he was not was a rock. A marshmallow, perhaps, but never a rock! Jesus saw him, however, not as he was, but as he would become.

Failure to accept him at face value. Until you totally accept your husband with no condition of change, it will be very difficult to admire him. The negative must be removed before the positive can be planted.

DEVELOPING ADMIRATION

One of a kind. All men are not the same. Each is a separate individual. His hobby can run the gamut from wild game hunting to needle point. How well do you really know your man? More and more I am impressed that God has given each man one woman who knows him intimately and can meet his needs. I don't need to know or understand my neighbor's husband or your husband—just my own. My husband is an individual, unlike any other man, and it is him I am to discover.

The questions on the next page are a tool to help you in learning to discover your man. I encourage you to write the answer to the questions on a sheet of paper. Then tonight ask your husband the questions and see how well you did!

1. What is the happiest thing that has ever happened to your husband?

2. What has been the hardest experience of his life?

3. What are his secret ambitions, his goals for his life?

4. What are his deep fears?

5. What about you does he appreciate the most?

6. What traits of yours would he like to see changed?

7. What man or men does he most admire?

Three years ago I asked my husband similar questions and found out I didn't know him nearly as well as I thought. I asked him to list some of his happiest times. He remembered a three-hour discussion we had in upstate New York, where he felt we communicated in a fantastic way. When I said, "What discussion?", he could not believe I didn't remember!

His second answer was "My first day at seminary." Now it was my turn to be flabbergasted. (It was then that I knew we would be returning to seminary for his doctorate!) I had been with him at seminary for four long years and had not grasped the significance of this experience in his life.

During the two-day seminar I give, called "How to be a Creative Counterpart," I ask the women to answer these questions and then ask their husbands for their answers. Amazing things have resulted. One woman wrote me the following note: "Last night I did what you asked us to. When we got to the question about his deepest fears in life, he began to open up and shared for the first time in our thirty years of marriage his fears about his business. We talked and cried together for three hours, and I'm convinced it was the beginning of a new marriage relationship for us."

The first suggestion for discovering your man has been to communicate with him. Too many married couples talk about trivia and never really get inside their partners to discover the joys, hurts, successes, and failures.

Wild game hunting or needle point? Take an interest in your husband's interests. That may sound easy, but for some of us it's not! My husband is interested in deep theological study, military history, and jogging. Jody tried unsuccessfully for nine years to get me out on the track. I had many good excuses: it was hot; I would perspire and ruin my hairdo; I couldn't make it around the track; I had too many things to do. One night he took my resting heart beat and it was eighty. Then, he took his, and it was fifty-seven. He explained to me that my heart was working harder than his, and thus I was wearing out faster.

That did it! It was off to the track! Know what? It's fun! It's fun because we do it together as a family. (Our three children can run a half-mile.) Secondly, I learned much about my husband and found many new things to admire about him. He has a fantastic build, and how many men can run three miles every day? (My appreciation climbed when I discovered how hard it was to run one mile, let alone three!) It has also been good for my figure. Jody is concerned about my heart. I'm concerned about my hips. Jogging helps both!

I have a dear friend whose husband is an avid fisherman. When they were newly married, he suggested they go fishing. Because she had heard that the family that plays together, stays together, she went. She recounted that the first time she put a minnow on a fishing hook, she was sure she would vomit. As with most things, it got easier, until soon she could do it without closing her eyes!

Now, many years and four children later, she is thankful she became interested in her husband's interests. She recently said, "Linda, do you know the best time Bruce and I had last year? It was at 6:00 A.M. cleaning fish by the lake. The children were asleep, and we talked of deep and wonderful things we rarely talk about as we cleaned the fish. I thanked God that morning that I had been willing to put that first minnow on the hook."

Are you listening? Can your husband talk to you and not be ridiculed? Can he confide in you and know his confidences will be safely guarded? Do you minimize his weaknesses and emphasize his manliness and his strengths? Do you create a climate in which he feels safe to voice his fears because you believe in him? Do you treat your husband as the most special person in the world or are you more polite to the neighbors? We teach our children to be polite, yet how polite are we to their fathers?

If you collapse on the couch, completely exhausted from a hard day, he's supposed to be understanding, isn't he?

Yet let an insurance salesman or a friend drop by, and we are instant smiles, coffee, and conversation! I'm not saying we should never "let our hair down" with our husbands, but some of us let it down and never roll it up again!

Wives often complain their husbands won't talk, but many times we fail to encourage them to talk. Often when talking to Jody, I sit with my yarn in my lap and crochet. One night he said, "Honey I'm tired of talking to your crochet hook! Do you have any idea how distracting it is to talk to someone who is always moving their hands ninety miles an hour?"

Draw him out. Set aside time each day to talk to him. Often I take an index card and write down all Jody is doing that day. As I pray for him, I refer to the card and feel like I'm vitally involved in each thing he does. At the end of the day, I am full of knowledgeable questions.

We have found that we talk better away from home. This may not be true for you. We love our home, but there are always interruptions: two phones ringing, three precious children needing attention, paper boys at the door to be paid, and many more. On our "dates," we go to a restaurant and sit and talk. We always find that we talk on a deeper level and communicate better away from the distractions of home. This technique may not be everybody's bag, so find something that works for you and do it!

Because many men have highly scientific or intellectually abstract professions, their wives say it is difficult to communicate with them about their work. I can sympathize. Many of Jody's abstract theological concepts are real mind-blowers! I find that when I'm really interested, however, I can understand almost anything. That's the key. I can also notice how absorbed he is in his subject, how he has mastered the intricate details, how he has worked out and developed his own ideas, and how loyal to them he is. Even when you can't totally understand all he is saying, you can look for character traits to admire.

Don't interrupt. This sounds simple, but many of us are guilty here. He begins, and we finish the sentence for him. After all, we know him so well that we are sure we know just what he is going to say! At other times, we are so wrapped up in what *we* want to say that we rudely interrupt to get our ideas across.

Learning to accept your husband's feelings, tastes, and attitudes can go a long way toward establishing the kind of communication we talk so much about. Does it matter whether acorn squash is good for him if he doesn't like it? Accept his tastes. He doesn't need a "dietician" or "substitute mother." Maybe he gets a kick out of football, and you feel the sport is stupid. Voice that opinion once or twice and what will you communicate? That you feel you married a stupid man. How willing do you think he'll be to express his likes and dislikes if he is called stupid when he does?

Forget the past. John comes home and says he has a fantastic land deal and is going to invest. Becky hysterically reminds him that their last real estate investment was a total and complete flop. "How can you think of doing it again? Don't you love me?" End of communication. John stomps into the other room and slams the door.

It's normal for a wife to have fears in an area where her husband has failed before, but how much better to have handled it like this. John says he has a fantastic land deal. Becky says, "Tell me more about it, John. It sounds exciting!" Beginning of conversation. John opens up and shares and his wife comments and asks more questions. She tells John she's happy he's found property he feels so good about. Later, she says, "You know, John, it's wonderful to have a husband I can lean on and trust. I know we both remember well the last investment fiasco, but I know you'll check into this one thoroughly. And I have confidence in your decision." Wow! This time John spends hours investigating the property. Why? Because he wants to live up to what Becky feels he is!

Let him dream. Many wives tramp through their marriages with hobnail boots, stepping on each and every dream. My husband said unexpectedly one night, "I'd like to go to Mt. Ararat and look for Noah's Ark." Immediately, a practical woman like me had to remind him that it would be terribly expensive, impossible for the children, and ridiculous for anyone but a professional climber.

Men like to dream. "Wouldn't it be fun to own a boat?" or "Let's take our savings and go around the world." Then practical wives fill in the reasons why it's impossible. The tragedy is not that so many husbands dream the impossible dream but that they quit dreaming altogether thanks to "practical" wives.

If you know your husband's dreams, you'll come a long way toward knowing him. If he feels free to express his dreams, it will help you become aware of him and his admirable qualities. Sometimes he just wants to bounce his ideas off someone. Does he feel free to do it with you or does he go to a business associate or another woman?

Have you ever considered how Sarah must have felt when Abraham decided to trade his mansion for a tent and go find a new land in a place he didn't know?

How do you suppose Mrs. Noah felt when Noah shared his dream of a big boat he wanted to build in the middle of the desert? It had never rained before on earth, and her husband wanted to build an ark for the coming flood!

How about Job's wife? What an encouragement she was! Job was totally defeated, physically ill, and trying to believe God and find the meaning in his suffering. In comes his wife, who says, "Curse God and die." Who needs encouragement like that?

An added tip from Jody: Don't say "always" and "never." "But, Honey, you *never* do that when I want you to," or, "Dear, you *always* do that the same way every year." These two words are like waving a red flag in front of a bull. They stop most conversations and start more quarrels than any other words in the dictionary.

Let's get specific. I have a close friend who is an adopted mother to me. She had been thinking much about admiring her husband of forty years and decided Thanksgiving would be the perfect time. Approaching him that morning she told him that on this Thanksgiving she was thankful for him, for his protective care of her all the years of their marriage, for his abundant provision, and for the security and satisfaction he had given her. She told him she was probably the most secure and protected woman in the world. She said her husband strutted around like a peacock the rest of the day. She had always admired her husband for the wrong things: his tenderness, thoughtfulness, and kindness.

Now tenderness, thoughtfulness, and kindness are godly and important qualities, but a man *also* needs to know that he is a man to you. That he is providing, protecting, and caring for you. As one woman put it, "Admire his masculinity!"

Keep these additional characteristics in mind as you seek to admire your husband: leadership ability, mental capacity, superior strength, sexual capacity, steadfastness, courage, logical mind, ability to handle finances, and athletic ability.

Your superstar. Take out a sheet of paper and write down every quality you can admire about your husband. List physical qualities, emotional, intellectual, and spiritual. Now that you know your husband's admirable qualities, why keep them to yourself? It's good to admire your husband secretly, but how much better to admire him actively! Reverence is putting your total partner acceptance into practice. So let's start practicing! No excuses. You've all made your lists and have lots of admirable qualities to choose from. Now it's simply a matter of opening your mouth and saying what you know to be true. You may feel awkward at first, but do it anyway!

Advice from a man. I asked a good friend, who has a *creative counterpart* for a wife, to list examples of the way his wife verbally shows her admiration for him and to express the way it makes him feel. He wrote the following:

> Joanne doesn't just tell me that I have a nice build, she says, "I love your wonderful body. I like to run my hands over the muscles in your back."
>
> Once when jogging together she said, "I was watching you run ahead of me. Your form is so effortless and graceful. No wonder I can't keep up with you." (The next day I knocked 1:5 minutes off my best time!)
>
> Late one evening, after a hard day, she said, "Thank you for working so hard to give us this home and all the material things we have. Sometimes I feel we just aren't appreciative enough of all you do." I could hardly wait to get to the office the next day!
>
> Not long ago we went over insurance, wills, and our financial situation. Joanne said, "I just can't believe how well you take care of me. You handle the present problems, which are plenty; but you even have our future planned."
>
> It's hard to express how her admiration makes me feel, to put it on paper, but it makes me want to be more of a man to her. It challenges me to grow (Lord knows I need it) to be stronger in my spiritual life. Maybe it's her, always working to perfect our relationship, that challenges me. She communicates by her admiration that she is truly interested in me as a person and in what I do. She makes me feel like a king.

What do *you* communicate to your husband? One wise woman put it like this: "I told *God* about his bad points, and told *him* about his good points."

THE EXECUTIVE VICE-PRESIDENT

Chapter Seven

A man walked into a library and asked the librarian for a copy of the book *Man the Master of Woman*. Without looking up, she pointed and said, "Sir, the fiction is in that corner."

Beginning in 1961 with the publication of *The Feminine Mystique*, there has been a re-examination of the numerous passages in the Bible regarding woman, her femininity, and the woman's role in the home. Particular scorn has been heaped upon the word *submission*. What is the woman's role? And more important, what does the Bible say about it?

There are three basic plans for marital happiness under consideration in our world today.

THREE MARITAL PLANS

PLAN A—THE PRESIDENT

Plan A says the decisions in the family should be made by the one who is most qualified. Plan A results in competition between husband and wife, and here is how it operates.[1]

The husband. He begins by *reasoning from confusion*. He has heard the rumor he is supposed to be the head of the home. However, after observing his wife's behavior he sees he is not getting any votes. Thus he begins to reason he is not the most qualified to make decisions (and in many areas he may not be). He can't act in confidence because he is not sure he will be supported by his wife. As a result, he *retreats* from leadership. Since every decision-making process ends in a battle and since he sees his wife is actually more qualified in some areas, he turns the reins over to her.

Gradually, however, he begins to *resent* his wife. He fumes internally over the fact that she will not respect his basic desire to lead the family. This ultimately comes to open *reaction*. Whenever she makes a mistake, he brings it to her attention. He now wants to prove she is wrong, and competition sets in. The end result of such a marriage is that all too frequently he *runs* elsewhere for total expression and fulfillment. He wants someone to respect him. He may find it in sports, other men, hunting, children, his business, or of course, another woman. This is often not out of a desire for sexual variety but out of an emotional need to be admired and respected.

The wife. She generally begins by *reasoning from pride.* She asks, "Who is most qualified?" And she answers, "I am." She sees her husband who is very human and who makes mistakes, and she wants to take over. As a result she *rejects* his leadership. She no longer encourages him to be the head of the home. Then paradoxically, when her husband seems uninterested in family involvement, she begins to *resent* him for not taking leadership. When she makes a wrong decision, she blames him. This leads to a strong *reaction* against his lack of leadership. She frequently *runs* elsewhere also. She buries her life in the children, women's Bible studies, outside involvement, or another man. Key word: *compete.*

PLAN B—THE HOUSEKEEPER

Plan B says the husband is the head or leader and yet the wife is not really a helpmate. She is not committed to being a *creative counterpart.* She is the woman who thinks marriage begins when you sink into his arms and ends with your arms in the sink. When the survey takers arrive at her door with their question, "And, Mrs. Smith, what is your occupation?" she sadly replies, "Oh, I'm just a housewife." As one woman aptly put it, "I'm a wife to a man, not a house!"

A woman caught in the housewife syndrome usually has some or all of the following characteristics: very dependent, little emotional control, very subjective, difficulty making decisions, and very passive. She is uninterested in growing as a person and feels her plight in life is to submit to a man, raise his children, and keep his house clean. She becomes boring as a person and lives in a dull routine. Often the television becomes her constant companion to help her escape from boredom. Because she is unfulfilled, she begins to *complain* and fits well into Solomon's description, "A nagging wife is like a dripping raindrop." She is the one who caused Solomon to say it is better to live in the corner of an attic than in a beautiful home with a contentious woman (Prov. 21:9).

The word that describes her is *complain,* and because she complains her husband usually complains, too—about her. And the couples in Plan B are caught in a vicious cycle that produces heartache and bitterness. Key word: *complain.*

PLAN C—CREATIVE COUNTERPART

God's plan for marital happiness involves a *spiritual head* and a *creative counterpart.* Instead of competing with each other as in Plan A and complaining to each other in Plan B, God's man and God's woman *complete* each other.

A *creative counterpart* is a helpmate, a compliment to her husband. She not only allows her husband to be the leader but encourages him to take the leadership by reverencing him and by being submissive to him. She has chosen to be submissive because God has commanded it and because she is convinced that only *completion* will result in a vital, fulfilling marriage.

She is submissive, but strives to be capable, intelligent, industrious, organized, efficient, warm, tender, gracious—all we saw in the beautiful blueprint in Proverb 31. She is not the President as in Plan A or the Housekeeper as in Plan B but the Executive Vice-President. Key word: *complete.*

THE MEANING OF HELPMATE

SLAVE OR COUNTERPART?

It is not a status of inferiority but a functional difference. The woman is in submission to her husband in the same way Christ is in submission to the Father. Yet Christ and the Father are equal and one! There cannot be two leaders. The purpose is functional teamwork that allows two people to complement one another instead of compete with one another in life.

Women sometimes say, "Don't say submission so loudly!" I hope to show you that submission is not a dirty word, but your hope of becoming all that God intended. Also, it's your *only* hope of your husband's becoming all that God intended —and all that you desire!

Christ is subject to God. He's equal to God, is very God, but is subject to the Father. Jesus, Creator of heaven and earth, submitted Himself to God and took His place in the chain of authority. It is no shame or dishonor for a woman to be under authority if the Lord Jesus was. Each marriage partner has a blessed, unique responsibility, a purpose in life that the other cannot possibly fulfill and cannot happily exist without.

Henry Brandt expressed it this way in a speech I heard recently; "The husband and wife are similar to the President and Vice-President (let's make that Executive Vice-President) of a bank. Both carry heavy responsibilities, help make policies, and live in accord with and are limited by the policies. On occasion, when a meeting of minds is impossible, the President must make the final decision. The husband is the head of the wife but the relationship should involve loyalty, good will, confidence and deep understanding."

One evening as we were seated around the dinner table, Joy, Robin, and Tommy entered into a "serious discussion" about who was the "boss" of the family. They talked back and forth and finally five-year-old Robin said, "I know. Daddy's the big boss and Mommy's the little boss!" The other two nodded approvingly. A pretty good explanation for a five-year-old!

YOUR ATTITUDE IS SHOWING

Submission is not only an action but an attitude. Many wives feel that when they exhibit an act or two that seems to indicate submission they've done their bit.

One writer says submissiveness is not a matter of mere outward form, but of inner attitude. A wife can be a person of strong opinions and still be submissive to her husband's authority if deep down she respects him and is quite prepared and content for him to make and carry out the final decision. On the other hand, a wife who scarcely opens her mouth with an idea of her own, never questions her husband's decisions may, underneath it all, nurse a deep and sullen rebellion.[2]

THE DIVINE IDEAL

The divine ideal for maximum marriage is summed up in Eph. 5:21–28. It is a beautiful picture and involves a husband and wife completing each other through assigned role relationships.

MUTUAL SUBMISSION

And be subject to one another in the fear of Christ. Wives, be subject to your own husbands, as to the Lord. For the husband is the head of the wife, as Christ also is the head of the church, He Himself being the Savior of the body. But as the church is subject to Christ, so also the wives ought to be to their husbands in every thing (Eph. 5:21–24, NASB).

Note the passage opens with the words, "and be subject to one another in the fear of Christ." This verse says that everyone is to submit, not just wives. (Good news!) What does it mean?

Prof. Howard Hendricks answers like this, "As members of the body of Christ, we all need each other. We are committed to each other because we are the family of God. By the control of the Holy Spirit, we are to subject ourselves to each other to willingly yield to the needs, decisions, and ideas of those with whom we are in daily contact. The *natural* thing is to demand our rights and to not submit to anyone; it is the *supernatural* thing to be unselfish and to submit to one another." [3]

A wife is to submit to her husband in everything. I asked my husband what total submission meant to him, and he said he could summarize it in two words—"no resistance." (Ouch!) He went on to explain that submission also carries with it the responsibility of a wife to tell her husband *exactly* how she feels on every issue of their life together, so there will be no misunderstanding. With an attitude of love, she should share her view with her husband. Her general approach should be something like this: "Honey, this is my viewpoint, and I ask you to consider it. The final decision, however, rests with you, and I will joyfully (that word is the killer) go along with whatever you decide." Some women will appear to go along with their husband's decisions, but will sulk or pout in silence. My husband says that's worse than words.

Our marriage is a partnership, but Jody is the head partner. Usually we agree on decisions, ideas, and goals, but no two partners always agree on everything. When I disagree with him, I lovingly present my reasons, then leave the final decision with him. This is *no resistance.* God knows what He is doing. If it turns out that I was correct and Jody's decision was wrong, God will let him know.

In our home, Jody is the disciplinarian. I almost always agree with the way he handles the children. We discuss it, read books together, and share all our ideas. Deep down, though, I'm an old softy, and the children know it. "Good old Mommy will always understand." There have been times when I have disagreed with the way the children should be disciplined and was overruled. At times it has been extremely difficult to go along *joyfully* with Jody's decision, without arguing in front of the children. Later, when I began to see the good effect of strong discipline, I was glad Jody had decided as he did.

Recently Jody and I had a financial decision to make concerning our marriage organization. We discussed our ideas and found we had totally opposite views. The more we talked, the more we disagreed!

Thus, Jody counseled with five mature Christian laymen and all five agreed with him. Six men on one side and me on the other! So after much prayer and consideration, Jody decided with the majority!

Never have I struggled so much with being *joyful*. In my will I accepted the decision but in my emotions I was screaming, "I'm right." I prayed often about my attitude and felt it was changing—that is, until I had my dream.

A week after Jody made this financial decision I dreamed he was put on trial and all the jurors proved him wrong and me right! I'd won! I awoke feeling sick to my stomach and said, "Oh God, I've tried in every way I know to give this to you and then I dream this dream. I again give it to you Lord, I *do* want to have the right response." My attitude gradually did change as I continued to claim God's promises.

There have been many situations in our marriage where Jody has changed his view when I've shared my ideas with him, but the issue is not who wins but how we respond.

The passage on submission sounds as if our husbands got together and wrote it, doesn't it? They didn't, but God did! Please note that God does not say your husband has earned the right to be your head or deserved it. He says that He, God, decided this was the best plan and therefore asks you to honor the plan. God had many plans available to Him and chose this one. And believe it or not, it's to your advantage!

So far this seems like a one-way street; the wife is to submit. But hold on. Your husband has an even greater responsibility: to love his wife *as Christ loved the church*.

A HUSBAND'S ALL-OUT LOVE

In the biblical view of marriage the submission of the wife is always set in the context of the total love of the husband.

> Husbands, love your wives, just as Christ also loved the church and gave Himself up for her; . . . So husbands ought also to love their own wives as their own bodies. He who loves his own wife loves himself; for no one ever hated his own flesh, but nourishes and cherishes it, just as Christ also does the church (Eph. 5:25–29, NASB).

The husband is to love his wife as Christ loved the church. (Right on, Paul. Preach it!) No one could ever measure a love that great. I'm ready for it—how about you? I can hear many of you saying, "This commandment wouldn't be so bad if my husband would love me as Christ loved the church and if he loved me as his own body. Maybe then submission would be a natural thing."

I personally believe it would become more natural. No woman will have difficulty with submission if she is being loved like that. I am blessed to have a godly husband who seeks to obey God and love me totally! You're right in thinking I have it easier than many of you. But at the same time God requires more of me in my response to Jody. To whom much is given, the Bible says, much will be required.

This passage does not say, "Be submissive to your husband if he is a wonderful, godly man," or "Be submissive on Mondays when you feel your husband deserves it." The text simply says, "Be submissive to your husband in everything. Period!" Now, don't close this book yet! It is obvious that this is the ideal. What about the practical, everyday reality? Many of us don't live with husbands who are trying to love as they should. The apostle Peter moves us out of the theory into the nitty-gritty.

CHRIST: OUR EXAMPLE

One of the most penetrating passages in all the Bible on

the subject of a submissive spirit, is found in 1 Pet. 2:18–3:7. The more I study it the more overwhelmed I become! Peter, while addressing men and women who were undergoing persecution for what they believed, exhorts them on the kind of godly responses they were to have in the midst of this situation. His advice is striking and contrary to what we might "intuitively feel" is fair. First he speaks of the submission of a servant (or, today, an employee) to an unreasonable master (employer).

> Servants, be submissive to your masters with all respect, not only to those who are good and gentle, but also to those who are unreasonable (2:18, NASB).

The issue in submission is *not* the qualifications of the one giving the orders or the reasonableness of his life. We are to respond to his position and not his personality. To always obey a leader or employer whom you like and agree with is very easy and contributes very little to the development of inner character. I find it easy to be submissive to Jody *when* he thinks I'm right; it's when he disagrees that it's hard!

> For this finds favor, if for the sake of conscience toward God a man bears up under sorrows when suffering unjustly (2:19, NASB).

The fundamental motivation in submission is *conscience toward God* and not the qualifications of the employer (or husband).

> For what credit is there if, when you sin and are harshly treated, you endure it with patience? But if when you do what is right and suffer for it you patiently endure it, this finds favor with God (2:20, NASB).

Now Peter says submission is simply part of our calling as Christians. Men must submit to employers (1 Pet. 2:18); children to parents (Eph. 6:1–4); all to government (1 Pet. 2:13); and wives to husbands (1 Pet. 3:1). Christ, he says, is the supreme illustration of this truth, and we are to follow in His steps.

> For you have been called for this purpose, since Christ
> also suffered for you, leaving you an example for you
> to follow in His steps (2:21, NASB).

Peter then enumerates the specific steps of submission Christ
followed.[4]

> Step 1. *Christ was without sin.* "Who committed no sin,
> nor was any deceit found in His mouth (2:22,
> NASB).

For Christ, sinlessness came by nature; for us it's obviously
not by nature but by confession. Peter says we are first of
all to check our heart attitudes for bitterness, resentment,
fear, anger rather than focus on the personality defects of
the one giving us the "orders."

> Step 2. *Christ blessed those who hurt him.* "And while
> being reviled, He did not revile in return; while
> suffering, He uttered no threats" (2:23*a*, NASB).

The Lord refused to retaliate with unkind words even though
He was spat upon and whipped. Even after they nailed Him
to the cross, He only said, "Father, forgive them, for they
know not what they do" (Luke 23:34, KJV).

Christ, in perfect love and submission to the Father, suffered for you and me! We see beautifully here the real test
of submission. It is not how others act toward you, but how
you respond. We are too concerned with the way other
people (husbands, for instance) act toward us. God does not
hold us accountable for our husband's actions, only for our
own.

Your husband may be wrong in a certain situation, and
God will deal with him in due time. God wants you to respond His way. What is His way? This leads us into step 3.

> Step 3. *Christ trusted the situation to the Father.* "But
> kept entrusting Himself to Him who judges
> righteously" (2:23*b*, NASB).

Jesus Christ committed Himself to God, who judges righteously. He was willing to rest His case with the Father. I am well aware that many times women live in intolerable home situations. God understands. He sees everything that happens, and he takes note of our reactions. We are never alone in the process of submitting to others.

Now why did Christ do this? If anyone ever had a right to complain that he was being unjustly treated, it was Jesus Christ! He had never sinned, and all the witnesses against Him could not agree upon a charge! What was His motivation?

Step 4. *Christ suffered that we might be healed.* "And He Himself bore our sins in His body on the cross, that we might die to sin and live to righteousness; for by His wounds *you were healed*" (2:24, NASB).

The ultimate goal of Christ's submission was that we might die to sin and live righteous lives—that we might be "healed." This is the ultimate goal for a wife in her submission to her husband. It is the only way to motivate him to be what God wants him to be.

Recently I talked to a man whose marriage had been somewhat shaky for a number of years. His wife had become a Christian and continually pressured him to be more interested in spiritual things and to change certain behavior patterns. The more she fought him, the more he reacted. Instead of motivating him to change, she was confirming his intention to remain exactly the same. Then she finally followed Christ's example and began to have a submissive spirit. Gradually he began to change and take a greater interest in spiritual things. He recently told my husband, "The turning point in our relationship was when Mary began to follow the Bible. The most beautiful thing in my life has been the silent pressure of a submissive wife."

Practical Peter now takes the example of Christ and applies it directly to the husband-wife relationship.

GOD'S WAY OF CHANGE

> *In the same way,* you wives, be submissive to your own husbands so that even if any of them are disobedient to the word they may be won *without a word* by the behavior of their wives (3:1, NASB).

"In the same way" refers us back to the example of Christ. Christ's submission to the Father involved unjust suffering at the hands of sinful men. Likewise, a wife's submission to her husband may involve unjust suffering while she is obeying Christ and submitting to her husband. But the same submissive spirit adopted by Christ is to be that of a wife to her husband *and* of a husband to his wife ("you husbands, *likewise.* . . .", 3:7). Futhermore, it is this kind of submissive spirit that is to exemplify the employee to his boss and the citizen to his government.

Note, this submission is to be *without a word.* Our normal tendency in correcting those over us is to be very verbal! We nag, cry, preach, pout, quote Bible verses, and drive our husbands further away. This is because we have forced him to defend himself. The disobedient husband is to be "won" (changed) by our behavior, not our words, our walk, or our talk! Oh, but it's so much easier to talk! Words are cheap. A godly quality of life is precious! What qualities are needed to bring about this change?

Peter says it clearly, "As they observe your chaste and respectful behavior" (3:2). An understanding of these two words in the Greek language is helpful in bringing them into twentieth-century focus. The word *chaste* comes from the Greek word *hagnos,* which means, according to Vine, "pure from every fault, immaculate." [5] In other words, a blameless life.

If you are walking without sin in your responses and if your husband observes a quality of life in you that is attractive, he will be drawn to it. Jesus said we are to be the salt of the earth. Salt makes people thirsty, thirsty for the quality of life Christ has given us.

Furthermore, the husband is to observe the *respectful* behavior. This is the same word used in Eph. 5:33 where Paul commands, "And let the wife see to it that she *respect* her husband." As we pointed out in the section under "Admiration," this means to respect and to admire. Thus, the two basic ingredients for bringing about a change in a disobedient husband are submission to his *authority* and consistent *admiration!* When a man receives this kind of treatment, coupled with unconditional *acceptance,* (the "three As"), watch out! Change is on its way! An application of the three As invariably results in motivating our husband to fulfill his potential! That's exciting! I have yet to meet a wife who consistently applied these three As whose husband didn't eventually start working on being what he should be!

Peter continues,

> And let not your adornment be external only—braiding the hair, and wearing gold jewelry, and putting on dresses; but let it be the hidden person of the heart, with the imperishable quality of a *gentle* and *quiet* spirit, which is precious in the sight of God (3:3–4, NASB).

Women throughout the centuries have focused on the external appearance, and Peter exhorts the wives to place greater emphasis on inward qualities of life. A key word is *only.* The external *is* important, but it is to be internal also. We *are* to make ourselves physically attractive to our husbands, but we are also, and with greater emphasis, to concentrate on a *gentle* and *quiet* spirit if we are to effect a change in a disobedient husband.

The word *gentle* comes from the Greek word *prautes.* It is a strong word for inner strength of character. Christ used it of his own disposition (Matt. 11:29). It refers to an attitude toward God in which we accept His dealings with us as good, and therefore without disputing or resisting. It is the kind of inner attitude that views all trials as a classroom of opportunity rather than a prison of circumstances.[6] A wife who has *prautes* is a wife who sees the hurt and trial forced upon her by a disobedient husband as tools in the hands of a loving heavenly Father to fashion her into a more perfect image of Himself. It involves a total lack of self-interest but strong inward control which wholly comes from a close walk with Christ. A man who is confronted with a wife possessing *prautes* is a man who comes under incredible divine pressure to change his way of life!

Peter also exhorts a wife living with a disobedient man to develop a quiet spirit (Greek, *hesuchios*). According to Vine this refers to a "tranquility arising from within, causing no disturbance to others." [7] Peter is *not* saying a submissive wife should never express herself. On the contrary, she should tell her husband *exactly* how she feels and believes on all decisions, but she is to do it with the inner strength of a quiet spirit.

A woman who lives in continual reaction to every hurtful or unjust thing her husband does is a woman who, in turn, causes her already wayward husband to react against her even more. She yells at the children, nags at him, and confirms him in his unbelief. Inner tranquility can *only* come from learning to trust the situation totally to the Lord, as Jesus did to His heavenly Father. It is the opposite of fear. A woman who trusts like this in the Lord experiences an inner calm and a freedom from fear, and isn't that what we all want? Peter makes this point in the following verses.

FEAR NOT!

> For in this way in former times the holy women also, who *hoped in God,* used to adorn themselves, being submissive to their own husbands (3:5, NASB).

Note the combination of "hope in God" and submission to their husbands.

> Thus Sarah obeyed Abraham, *calling him lord,* and you have become her children if you do what is right *without being* frightened by any fear. (3:6, NASB).

How did Sarah obey Abraham? She *hoped in God* and called Abraham lord. In other words, her trust was not in Abraham but in God. She trusted herself into the hand of God and then obeyed her husband. That is following in Christ's steps (2:23).

Sarah obeyed Abraham and called him her master. But then an Old Testament saint like Abraham was probably the perfect husband, right? Not on your life! Once while traveling in Egypt, Abraham feared for his life when he heard the Pharaoh had his eye on Sarah. So to save his own skin, he told the Pharaoh that Sarah was his sister, not his wife. The Pharaoh then proceeded to take Sarah into his harem! Did Sarah scream "rape?" Did she cry, kick, or throw a tantrum? No. Trusting God, she submitted to Abraham's pathetic plan and went into the Pharaoh's harem. Most of us would never sit still for such a thing, but Sarah knew God would work it out, somehow. So she waited. In a dream, God told the Pharaoh that Sarah was Abraham's wife and warned him of impending wrath. The Pharaoh was so terrified of Abraham's God, he took Sarah to Abraham and asked them to leave the country immediately. Sarah gave God time to work in the situation—and He did! She placed her trust in God, and therefore did not give way to fear.

If the Pharaoh had come to Sarah to have sexual relations, she would have been forced to tell him the truth, but God never allowed that situation to happen. He intervened and solved the problem Himself. Most of us are so quick to open our mouths that we never give God a chance to work.

Peter says we are Sarah's daughters if we do what is right and do not give way to fear (3:5–6). But we *are* afraid. There are four basic reasons why women are afraid to submit to the authority of their husbands.

1. *We're afraid of what he might do or ask us to do.* The first thing many women say when hearing about submission is, "But he'll ask me to mate swap." It's true that there are husbands who ask their wives to do horrible things, and I

hope to answer some of their questions in the next chapter under the limits of submission. For most of us, however, questions like this are a scapegoat. What we're really afraid of is that he might ask us to do several things that we just don't want to do!

2. *We're afraid he will fail.* It's possible, of course, that God wants your husband to fail occasionally, since we grow most through trials and failure. One of the hardest things I've ever had to do was step out of the way and let my husband fail. I try hard to say "God, he's yours. I love him and don't want him to ever be hurt, but Lord, don't let me get in Your way. If this trying situation is for his growth, let me love him and encourage him and stand behind him, but keep me out of Your way." I have to fight my tendency to be the "mother" and to step in and take over when the going gets rough!

3. *We're afraid of his irresponsibility.* To simply yield everything to your husband when his past track record is one of never assuming responsibility for what you yield up naturally creates much fear. What will happen to me? To the children? There may be situations in which you should gradually begin to turn things over to him. To dump it on him all at once could overwhelm him. But frequently, the reason a man fails to assume responsibility is because he is not receiving a loving dose of the "three As."

Once the responsibility is clearly his and he sees you are not going to fight him about every point on a particular issue anymore, more often than not, he will begin to feel the weight of that responsibility and assume it. Then, as he assumes it, if he finds you consistently admiring him when he takes a step and unconditionally accepting him when he makes a mistake, he will be motivated to develop his potential!

In the event his irresponsibility continues to the point that the marriage is ruined, it could be God's way of taking him out of your life. Even then a wife can disobey with a submissive spirit and communicate acceptance. However, our focus always tends to be on the *what if*. As I said before, I have never met a woman who faithfully applied the "three As" who ever had to face this kind of situation. Let's keep our focus on trusting God and loving our husbands rather than on *how long?* and *what's my out?*

4. *We are afraid of God's will.* Many women will agree with everything that has been discussed above, but when it comes to applying it in real life, a different fear surfaces. It is the fear that God may allow the situation to go on for too long or that He might allow too intense a hurt to occur. In effect, it is a fear of God's will and a lack of trust in Him. It is almost as if we view God as unconcerned about us, as if He really doesn't love us. After all, He would never cause me to have to make such choices if He really loved me!

God has clearly demonstrated His love in sending His only Son to die for us, so there is no question of His love. If the hurt were to continue for a long time and if it were to be intense, there is no one who is more grieved than our heavenly Father. Yet if He allows it, it is clearly for our ultimate good (Rom. 8:28). From God's viewpoint, the trials we go through are not nearly as important as the responses we make to them.

Sharon was a beautiful, intelligent woman and a new Christian when her husband left her and moved to another state to enjoy wine, women, and song. Many called her a fool during the years she waited and loved him and strived to be submissive in spite of her circumstances. She shared this beautiful quote from Alan Redpath which she memorized and claimed during that difficult time.

> There is nothing—no circumstance, no trouble, *no testing*—that can ever touch me until, first of all it has gone past God and past Christ, right through to me. If it has come that far, it has come with a *great purpose,* which I may not understand at the moment. But as I *refuse* to become panicky, as I lift up my eyes to Him and accept

it as coming from the throne of God for some *great purpose* of *blessing* to my own heart, no sorrow will ever disturb me, no trial will *ever* disarm me, no *circumstance will cause me to fret*—for *I shall rest in the joy of what my Lord is!*—That is the rest of victory! [8]

Many who rose in horror and wailed "fool" became silent when her husband returned and deeply committed himself to her and the children.

These "four fears" comprise the biggest single barrier to submission. They are real and cause many sincere women great emotional distress. However, they must be set against the background of a loving heavenly Father who is the blessed controller of all things. God is alive and well today! He is not just an abstract theory but a living Person who actually invades lives and changes situations, protects his children, and gives comfort. The whole Bible testifies to this. Let's start taking our Christianity seriously. It is a supernatural faith!

BARRIERS, BENEFITS AND LIMITS

Chapter Eight

To some, regardless of *how* it is said, submission will not be accepted! Christ was called a fool when he hung on a cross and suffered to heal you and me. Today, some would stand and call the woman a fool who suffered to heal her husband. In our society you don't yield your rights, you cling to them and fight for them. As the beautiful song says, "Christ could have called ten thousand angels to destroy the world and set him free." A wife *can* call ten thousand lawyers to defend her and set *her* free. Each of us has a choice.

God never said submission was easy (and I agree), but He did say of all the plans available to Him, the plan He chose of *spiritual head* and *helpmate* was the most perfect for the physical, emotional, and spiritual welfare of both partners!

Let's look at some of the barriers to a submissive spirit, as well as some of the benefits and limits of submission.

BARRIERS TO A SUBMISSIVE SPIRIT

BARRIER 1—THE DISOBEDIENT HUSBAND

First let me say I rarely meet an obedient wife! As pointed out, any wife who faithfully applies the "three As" (*acceptance, admiration,* submission to his *authority*) will almost inevitably see her husband begin to change. Our problem is that we want push-button results, the American way, after applying a few principles for a week or so. Let me emphasize we are applying these principles in order to "follow in His steps" and *not* in order to effect a change in our husbands. We are doing these things because it is part of being a Christian and not in order to get our husbands to change.

If our motivation is to effect a change in our husband and if after applying the "three As" for a brief time we see no change, obviously our motivation to continue will fade. As one woman said to me, "Oh, I've tried all of that, and it didn't work." Actually she had tried it for a week or so and only halfheartedly at that. Furthermore, her efforts were all external; inwardly her spirit was full of resentment and bitterness.

BARRIER 2—THIS IS ARBITRARY DISCRIMINATION BASED ON SEX

Why should the woman be the one who should always have to "submit"? Why can't it be mutual? First of all, let me say that in the biblical view of marriage, it *is* mutual. The wife is to fully express her views, disagree anytime she feels it, and they should mutually come to decisions agreed upon by both. This is always the case in a marriage that is truly Christian, because the word *submission* is set in the context of the husband loving the wife as Christ loved the church. A woman who is being loved by a man in such a way that he puts her interest, desires, and dreams, above his own and who is dead to himself and gives to her, hardly has any trouble being submissive. That is the true biblical picture of marriage.

But secondly, we must admit that this arrangement *is* arbitrary discrimination based on sex. However, it is *not* unjustly arbitrary. Everything God does is for the best for His children. He set it up this way, because in His infinite love and wisdom He knows this is the best arrangement. On what other terms would you suggest the *head* and *helpmate* be determined? On who is "most qualified"? If that were the basis, there would be nothing but debate on who is the most qualified on every point, and marriage would end up in perpetual competition instead of completion. God's way is totally unrelated to the basic qualifications or intrinsic merits of the husband and wife. It is a purely functional set-up, as in a corporation chain of command.

BARRIER 3—A SQUELCHING OF PERSONAL IDENTITY

Some have argued that such a view of marriage "de-humanizes" women and results in a total loss of personal identity. It is to become submerged in "some man," and as a result, American housewives are not able to "find out who they really are." However, in view of the fact that biblical submission is set in the context of the husband loving his wife as Christ loved the church, it is hard to see how such a loss of identity could take place.

My husband desires that I be the most fulfilled woman alive! He would do almost anything in order to help me find my identity. But beyond that, many women in this situation of submerged identity are that way not because they have submitted to their husbands, but because they have not made any attempts to reach out, develop outside interests, meet people, and develop their minds. Instead they have stayed around the house all day watching soap operas and playing with (or screaming at) small children.

Paradoxically, Jesus says one does not find personal identity by demanding rights and rejecting the biblical view of marriage. On the contrary, "For whoever wishes to save his life shall lose it; and whoever loses his life for My sake and the gospel's shall save it" (Mark 8:35, NASB). We find our identity not by focusing on "who we are" but by a denial of ourselves. Out of death comes real life! A woman finds her identity by denying herself for her husband and her children and other people. A man finds his identity by denying himself and living for his wife and children. It is in self-denial that true inward qualities are wrought and a beautiful life is developed.

BARRIER 4—THE FOUR FEARS

The "four fears" were discussed in the last chapter under

1 Pet. 3:5–6. They are (1) fear of what our husband might ask us to do; (2) fear of our husband's failure; (3) fear of his irresponsibility; and (4) fear of God's will. Together, they constitute a formidable obstacle.

BARRIER 5—PRIDE

This barrier is perhaps the most common of all. We always tend to think we can do a better job! Our views are superior. When a husband and wife disagree, it often becomes a point of pride in the wife that she always knows better. For example, let's say the husband wants to discipline the children in a certain way. How often have you retorted, "What do you know about it? I'm home with the children all day, and I know what they need better than you do!"

A man faces this daily with his employer. When he and his boss disagree as to how things should be done, it often becomes a pride problem. Far better for both the wife and the employee to forcefully and freely express their views and leave the decision up to the husband or employer rather than make a continual contest out of it. If your husband makes a wrong decision and should have followed your counsel, that is now between him and God, and he dosen't need an "I told you so" spirit emanating from his *creative counterpart!*

THE BENEFITS OF A SUBMISSIVE SPIRIT

The first benefit is that you glorify God by being obedient to His commandment. That is exciting, and there are practical benefits for us right where we live, too!

TENSION RELEASER

I believe submission is one solution to tension, tiredness, and pressure. Many a woman's tension, tiredness, and headaches are a result of absorbing responsibilities God never intended her to have.

Mary and Chuck were a couple locked in the cycle of competition. She felt responsible for every decision from the family business which they ran together to the clothes he wore! She pressed, connived, and pressured to get her way. The right decision was *her* decision.

The stress and tension Mary experienced showed on her face. She hated the word *submission* and fought against any plan that said she was not the leader.

After attending the Creative Counterpart Seminar, Mary did an about-face. She saw God and the beauty of His plan and made a commitment to be submissive to her husband. She actually made her commitment in the form of a contract with God, and here it is.

I, today, Wednesday, November 20, vow to myself, not to suggest, tell, nag, or criticize my husband on how to run his business. I will bite my tongue, leave the premises or do whatever is necessary, so as not to force my opinion. My knowing that my opinions are right will be satisfaction enough—no one else need share how smart and terrific I really am! I am now willing to accept his business failure to enforce this rule! I will read this each day before I start work. If I should fail to achieve this goal even twice, I will quit my job knowing it is a hindrance to my becoming a *creative counterpart.*

Mary recently told me that "life has changed from 'totally serious' to 'fun and enjoyable.' I never realized the pressure and tension I was under."

HUSBAND CHANGER

Submission is the only hope of changing your husband. Your husband will change as you allow him to be head of his home and are submissive to him. He will not change by your nagging, belittling, suggesting, reminding, or mothering.

Jody and I were married as college students. I had worked while in college, had a scholarship, and knew that money was hard to come by! Jody had not worked and did not know that money was hard to come by! Guess who was more responsible with the finances? Guess who let it be known that she was more responsible? Innumerable arguments resulted from my desire to know how every penny was spent. Jody, a book addict, finally began to "smuggle" books he had purchased into the house and put them on the shelf where I wouldn't see them. When I did find the book and asked him if it were new, he would smile and say, "Oh, no, Honey. I've had it for months!"

Later, when I began to understand what God wanted me to be as a wife, I totally let go of the finances. It was done with fear and trembling, but it was done! I was submissive to Jody and began to pray that God would make him faithful in this area.

Today, Jody is so faithful with our finances, I sometimes wonder if I prayed the right prayer! We are free from debt, pay cash for our purchases, and have a detailed budget. We have several credit cards but rarely use them. Jody's policy is, "Don't buy it until you have the money," and I respect him greatly for it. The tables have been turned, and now it's me coming to him to ask forgiveness for charging a dress that was on sale! Jody speaks often at seminars on the subject of finances and instructs other men how to be financially faithful. This was the man I didn't trust with a dime!

One woman who became a Christian after several years of marriage realized that her marriage was a case of total role reversal. She was the leader and her husband the helper. She was aggressive and outgoing and he was not. After struggling to discern what God wanted to do in her marriage, she decided to be submissive to her husband, even though she feared he wouldn't lead. Later, she wrote me,

> I really believe a Christian man can't be the man God intended until his wife is submissive and fits in with his plans. As I'm learning to do this, Mike is getting more confidence. We really share and talk more. In intimate matters, things are much improved. I realized that I hadn't been meeting his needs in any way. I'm convinced that if wives will go to the Lord, ask Him to

make us submissive, and then obey (that's what hurts), then the Lord will really make our homes the picture of Christ and the church!

YOUR FULFILLMENT

I believe submission is the only way to true fulfillment as a woman. You may have been in warfare for years and it has cost you everything: someone to lead you, security, and inner peace. You may have gotten your way in some areas, but it has cost you a relationship with your man now and after the children are gone.

YOUR SEXUAL RESPONSE

Submission is many times a key to sexual response. According to a survey we personally conducted among two thousand Christian women, 39% of those who had been married twenty years indicated they have experienced an orgasm sometimes, rarely or never. This is one of the most common problems women bring to marriage counselors. The reason is that sexual response at the physical level is the equivalent of submission at the psychological level. Men and women tend to view sexual intercourse from a different perspective. A man tends to see it as a "taking" or a "possessing." A woman, on the other hand, tends to conceptualize it as a "yielding up" of herself. Obviously, if a woman does see sexual intercourse as a yielding up and if she is in continual rebellion and disobedience to her husband, it will carry over to the marriage bed and can block her ability to respond.

THE LIMITS OF SUBMISSION

You recall the story of Abraham and Sarah. She was obedient to him but did not actually sin herself. If the Pharaoh had come in to sleep with her, she should not have agreed, for that would have been her own personal sin.

In Acts 5:1–8 we read the story of Ananias and Sapphira.

Together this husband and wife sold a piece of land and agreed together to lie about the amount they gleaned from the sale. The husband came in alone and lied to the disciples and immediately fell dead. Three hours later, his wife came in, and as pre-arranged, repeated the same lie. The apostle Peter said to her, "How could you agree to test the Spirit of the Lord?" And she, too, fell dead.

Some have said that a woman who is totally submissive to her husband is not responsible to God if he causes her to sin. This passage proves otherwise. Each human being is responsible for his or her own sins. The limit of submission is this: total submission, without personal sin.

WHEN CAN I DISOBEY?

1. When your husband asks you to do something directly contrary to Scripture. Remember that your conscience is not always a reliable guide and neither is what you feel the Lord is leading you to do. Go strictly by the Book!

2. When you have worked through the following program:[1]
- Ask "What is the need in my husband's life behind the request he is making?"
- Suggest a creative way of meeting that basic need without resorting to contradicting Scripture.
- Trust God as Sarah did. God may want to intervene and demonstrate His power.

Suppose for instance a husband asks his wife to get an abortion, and she feels this is wrong. First, is abortion contrary to Scripture? Some Christians believe it is and others believe it isn't. For the sake of our example, let's assume that this particular woman believes the Bible is against abortion.

Secondly, she would ask, "What is the need in my husband's life behind asking me to have an abortion?" Perhaps the couple has several children already and the husband is afraid of having another to provide for. Perhaps the wife is no longer a wife, but only a mother, and the husband views the child as another threat. Perhaps he's afraid of losing his job, and feels it's no time to have a child. There could be many reasons.

After discerning the basic need, the wife should suggest a creative way of meeting that basic need without resorting to contradicting Scripture. Perhaps she could admit her failure as a wife, ask forgiveness, and show him what a fantastic wife she can be! If money were the issue, perhaps she could offer to bring in additional income. We can all be creative if we get our minds out of their ruts and try!

I offer these limits of submission because I realize that bizarre situations can occur. I am in no way saying that you should not be submissive to your husband! Probably 99 percent of you would never seriously have to work through these questions. I include them for the 1 percent. We need to remember that our emotional focus should be on being submissive, not "Where is my out?"

A REAL BEAUTY

We read in 1 Peter 3 that a woman should have "the unfading beauty of a gentle and quiet spirit, which is so precious to God." The Greek word for *precious* is used two other times in 1 Peter. First, that the shed blood of Jesus Christ is precious, and second, that He is the precious cornerstone of our faith. The third time it is in reference to a godly, submissive woman. God says we, too, can be precious as the Lord Jesus is. That a calm and gentle, submissive spirit is rare and costly and of great worth to God. If you have ever met a woman such as this, you have not forgotten her! She is precious to God, a glory to her hubsand, and a joy to be around!

MY BELOVED AND MY FRIEND

Chapter Nine

During a recent seminar in Missouri, I told the women we were going to discuss being creative lovers, and one woman said quite loudly, "Whoopee!" I hope you, too, are as eager to learn about this important area of your marriage!

Today, we are all bombarded with the world's view of sex. In fact, we can't miss it! What many of us are missing is God's view of sex. And he has many interesting things to say on the subject! The Bible discusses sex openly and matter-of-factly, considering it a precious gift from God. We all have ideas, opinions, fears, frustrations, inhibitions, and guilt that have accumulated over our lifetimes. Romans 12:2 says, "Do not be conformed to this world, but be transformed by the renewing of your mind" (NASB). Stop right now and ask God to give you a clean mental slate. He will help you put aside all preconceived ideas. Only then will you be ready to hear what He has to say. God wants to renew our minds in every area—including sexual attitudes.

EXCHANGING GIFTS

Let the husband fulfill his duty to his wife, and likewise also the wife to her husband. The wife does not have authority over her own body, but the husband does; and likewise also the husband does not have authority over his own body, but the wife does. Stop depriving one another, except by agreement for a time that you may devote yourselves to prayer, and come together again lest Satan tempt you because of your lack of self-control (1 Cor. 7:3–4, NASB).

Paul is saying your body is a gift to your husband and his body is a gift to you. Our bodies are to be given to each other willingly to please one another. In a sense, Paul is saying a husband and wife should be totally available to his or her partner. He also said, "Stop depriving one another, except to devote yourself to prayer." My husband says he has heard of women giving many excuses to avoid sex, but never prayer!

The above passage shows us the equality God wants in the sexual relationship. Many wives have been taught a distorted concept of a woman's sexual nature. They have been told that a woman, "by nature," has less sexual drive than a man, is less passionate, is less frequently and intensely aroused, and that strong sexual desire and satisfaction are not a part of her nature.

Certainly men and women differ in their sexual responses, just as they differ in anatomy and physiology. But the pleasure and satisfaction experienced by a normal woman, while different from that of her husband, is at least as deep and profound. Her sex drive is also equally strong. If, in fact, we could compare the magnitude of response, there are a number of reasons we might expect to find her drive stronger, and her satisfaction greater. "The sexual vigor of a healthy, erotically awakened woman is very great; in fact, it may be greater than the potency of the average man."[1]

GET INTOXICATED!

Drink from your own well, my son—be faithful and true to your wife. Let your manhood be a blessing; rejoice in the wife of your youth. Let her charms and tender embrace satisfy you. Let her love alone fill you with delight (Prov. 5:15, 18–19, TLB).

A beautiful parallel is drawn here between thirst quenched by drinking cool, fresh water and a couple's sexual thirst being satisfied by regular, exciting sexual union in marriage.

The phrase "rejoice in the wife of your youth" indicates

that the sexual relationship is to provide the marriage partners great pleasure. The wife is described as tender, charming, loving, and satisfying.

My favorite translation of this passage is, "Let your love and your sexual embrace with your wife *intoxicate* you continually with delight. Always enjoy the *ecstasy* of her love." What a picture! Intoxicate and ecstasy! I fail to see, here, the poor, enduring wife who puts up with her husband's sexual advances. I see an exciting, highly erotic, and loving relationship. Since this picture of marriage is from God's Word, it's a good bet that this is what He has in mind for *your* marriage!

SOLOMON'S BEST SONG

The Song of Solomon contains eight chapters of beautiful poetry, picturing the love relationship between husband and wife. It describes in vivid, poetic language the physical bodies of married lovers, techniques in sexual arousal between husband and wife, the feelings, the attitudes, the imaginations, the dreams, and the spiritual and sexual joys they experience.[2] For a better understanding of the Song of Solomon, read my husband's excellent book *Solomon on Sex* (Thomas Nelson, 1977)!

Solomon's Song is the story of the King of Israel, who wooed and won the Shulammite, a lovely country maiden, as his wife. Each passage is packed with abundant lessons from God on the sexual aspects of marriage.

COMPLIMENTS AND OTHER GOODIES

"Like an apple tree among the trees of the forest, so is my beloved among young men" (Song of Sol. 2:3, NASB). Solomon and his bride are actively involved in lovemaking in this passage. Since the apple is a very frequent symbol in the Near East for love, it is used throughout the Song to symbolize sexual love. She is praising his lovemaking ability and telling him what a fantastic lover he is.

You may not think of your husband as the last of the red-hot lovers, but *he* wants you to! A man's ego is intricately tried up in his ability as a lover, and your rejection can scar him deeply. We have the idea that women are the sensitive ones, but I believe a man is more sensitive when it comes to sex! If you think he is a boring, run-of-the-mill lover, that's probably just what he'll be! He needs and wants to hear your praise! Tell him you find his body attractive, that his desire to please you is exciting, and that you like the way his hands are so gentle and yet so strong. Every man longs to hear, "Honey, you're a fantastic lover!" or, "I feel sorry for every other woman in the world because they don't have you for a lover!"

Perhaps you're thinking, "Oh, brother! There is absolutely nothing sexy about that klutz I'm married to!" Oh, yes there is. There is always *something* you can praise him for! Never be deceptive, but creatively search for the positive qualities. Verbalize your praise. He'll love it!

STATE YOUR PREFERENCE

Solomon and his bride continue with their lovemaking. She says, "Sustain me with raisin cake, refresh me with apples, because I am lovesick" (2:5, NASB).

By saying she is sick or weak with love, she means she is completely overcome with sexual desire. She therefore asks Solomon to sustain her with raisin cakes and apples (symbols of erotic love). In other words, she is asking him to satisfy her sexually without delay!

His wife then tells Solomon exactly how he can satisfy her. "Let his left hand be under my head and his right hand embrace me (2:6, NASB). This suggests she desires him to fondle and stimulate her body. Please take note! They are communicating during their lovemaking—openly, unashamedly, and freely. Solomon explains what he is doing to please her and asks what else he can do to satisfy her. Many men and women don't know how to please their mates because they have what I call "silent sex."

A lady came in for counseling and said that after twenty

years of marriage she had never experienced an orgasm. The counselor asked if she had ever told her husband how to stimulate her. She said, "Oh, of course not."

LOOK IN THE MIRROR

In chapter 4 we have the second love scene. Solomon praises his wife's physical appearance, starting at the top and working downward, probably caressing her as he speaks. He says she has eyes like doves; her hair is long and black; her teeth smooth and white; her lips, red and lovely; her cheeks, fair; her neck, erect; her breasts, full and youthful; her garden (genitals), erotically scented.

Throughout the Song of Solomon, poetic language is used to describe the genitalia. The "garden" refers to the female genitals and the "fruit" to the male genitals.

What is your husband's picture of you? Is he aware of your feminity, that you are an exciting woman and his lover, or are you just his children's mother and his housekeeper? Does he consider you attractive? Look at the women in an average neighborhood. It's a tragedy that so many women stop caring about their appearances as soon as they get that MRS! Let's get personal. Do you care as much now about your appearance as you did before you were married?

I have a friend whose husband is a pilot and is often home for days at a time. One morning she went into the bathroom about nine and spent an hour taking a shower, shaving her legs, powdering, perfuming, dressing, and fixing her hair. She walked into the living room, and her husband said, "Where are you going?" When she told him she had her yearly appointment with her gynecologist, he said, "Gosh. I wish you'd get dressed up like that for me sometimes!"

Most of us are embarrassed when we journey to the gyne- cologist's office, so we groom ourselves perfectly from head to toe in order to compensate. (I'm sure a survey of doctors would reveal that they rarely see a woman with unshaven legs!) It's a sad irony that many of us dress fit to kill for comparative strangers, but look like early-American washer-women for our husbands.

Do you seek by your physical appearance to please your husband? I found out after several years of marriage that Jody wasn't wild about my abundance of red, white, and blue outfits. He likes very bright colors and pastels. So who do I dress to please—the editors of *Harper's Bazaar* or my husband?

Jody likes thin women—a tragedy for me since I love to eat! My view of heaven is a banquet table with delicacies available continuously. Because of this, through blood, sweat, tears, and Weight Watchers, I lost twenty pounds! Recently Jody put his arms around me and said "Honey, I love your new body."

One wise woman told me she always freshens her makeup and hair and, if necessary, changes her clothes before her husband arrives home. "After all," she said, "He looks at women who strive to be attractive all day at the office. Shouldn't I try as hard?"

I've asked Jody to call me before he leaves work, so I have fifteen minutes to prepare myself physically, emotionally, and spiritually. That may mean changing the blouse that Tommy has smeared peanut butter on, or quickly picking up toys. More often, though, it means giving my day to God again, asking Him to help me get my eyes off myself and onto Jody. I ask God to make me sensitive to Jody's needs when he walks in the door. How I can meet those needs? Sure, I share all the joys and frustrations of my day with Jody, but first I try to concentrate on him, saving my needs for later.

EXCUSES, EXCUSES

In chapter 5, we enter a scene where Solomon comes to his wife late at night, eager to make love, and his wife gives the great grand-daddy of all excuses. "I have taken off my dress, how can I put it on again?" (5:3a, NASB). This indicates she is undressed and ready for bed. As was the custom, the door was locked. In order to unlock the door and let Solomon in, she would have to get up, put on a robe, and walk across the room. In effect she's saying, "Oh, Solomon, can't it wait? Can't you see I'm tired and all ready for bed?"

Then she comes up with another excuse, "I have washed my feet, how can I dirty them again?" (5:3b, NASB) Since it was a religious ritual to wash your feet before going to bed, she is saying, "Not only would I have to put on my robe and walk across the room, but I'd even have to rewash my feet!"

How do you respond to your husband's lovemaking? Do you respond with eagerness, joy, and tenderness, or do you avoid it as often as possible and endure it when you have to? Are any of these excuses familiar?

1. Sudden headache.

2. Too tired. (You *are* tired! You've been doing things for people all day, and now you want to crawl under the sheets and be left alone!)

3. Saying no as punishment. Is sex a favor you bestow or withhold according to whether or not you are pleased with him?

Are you remembering past wrongs? Has he been unfaithful and that keeps coming back to your mind each time he wants to give love to you? I don't mean to minimize the hurt and anguish a wife feels if her husband has been unfaithful, but if you dwell on it, you'll destroy yourself and your marriage.

Apply 1 Corinthians 13 to your sexual relationship. Is it patient and kind; never envious or jealous; not possessive; not conceited or rude; never indiscreet; does not insist on its own way; not self-seeking; never touchy or resentful; pays no attention to a suffered wrong; does not count up past wrongs; always believes the best of him; never fails?

We are not capable of that kind of love by ourselves. But with God all things are possible. Remember, God is at work within you every day, conforming you to the image of Christ.

I continually see women who make excuses to avoid their husbands physically. If you are one of these women, four things are likely to happen in your marriage:

1. *Your husband will react.* He may try slight pressure at first, then apply force, causing terrible problems in your relationship. After putting up with countless excuses, one husband finally confronted his wife, "You are a good mother, a good cook, and a good housekeeper. You're attractive and socially poised. But, Baby, I need a *woman!*" With that statement, he walked out the door for the last time.

2. *Your husband will let you have your way, silently resenting you.* Your relationship will suffer disastrous consequences. One wife said, "My husband leaves me alone. He only approaches me once a month and that's the way I like it."

What kind of love relationship is that? What kind of marriage can you have when both partners avoid each other for fear of a fight over sex? The wife sleeps on one side of the bed and the husband on the other, hoping their big toes never touch because the other might think it was a sexual advance! This is not a marriage at all. It's two strangers occupying the same dwelling.

3. *You'll tempt him to adultery.* If you have shattered his ego by constant refusal or played the "dutiful wife who endured him sexually," you have left him open to the sweetness and tenderness of another woman. To prove to himself that he is attractive and desirable as a man, he might seek out a woman who will make him feel loved. If he commits adultery under these circumstances, you are also guilty.

4. *You'll be out of fellowship with God.* The Bible says clearly that you do not have authority over your own body in marriage but that your husband does. The same is true of his body. If either of you has usurped that authority, you have disobeyed God.

DELIGHTFUL DAYDREAMING
    Solomon's wife describes her husband physically:
    My beloved is dazzling and ruddy, outstanding among
    ten thousand. His head is like gold, pure gold; his locks
    are like clusters of dates, and black as a raven. His eyes
    are like doves, beside streams of water, bathed in milk,
    and reposed in their setting. His cheeks are like a bed
    of balsam, banks of sweet-scented herbs; His lips are
    lilies, dripping with liquid myrrh. His hands are rods of
    gold set with beryl; his abdomen is carved ivory inlaid
    with sapphires. His legs are pillars of alabaster set on
    pedestals of pure gold; his appearance is like Lebanon,
    choice as the cedars. His mouth is full of sweetness.
    And he is wholly desirable. This is my beloved and this
    is my friend (5:10–16, NASB).

Solomon is not present. His wife is daydreaming about her
husband, her lover and friend. What a perfect combination!
She pictures him in her mind and concludes he is wholly
desirable. Her thoughts of him are very physical, and she
anticipates his return.
    How do *you* think about your husband? Is he that nice
man who brings home the paycheck, goes to church, and
plays with the children? That's fine, but it's not enough!
Think back. How did you think of him before you were
married? I'm sure you noticed and thought about his physique
—his strong hands and the way it felt so good when he put
his arms around you. You noticed the straightness of his
shoulders, the smile that told you he longed to have you as
his own. It sent chills up your spine. After you live with
someone for several years, however, you stop noticing. In
fact, some of us begin to notice only the *bad* things and tease
him about his pot belly and balding hair!
    I'll never forget an experience I had at a university. I had
been invited to speak to a group of college girls, and was
first enjoying a luncheon with them. When it was time for
me to speak, I was introduced as Linda Dillow, and before

another word could be spoken, a cute little eighteen-year-old piped up and said, "Oh, are you Jody Dillow's wife? I think he's wonderful!" The last sentence was said with a sort of swoon. She went on to talk about my husband as if he were Tarzan, Albert Einstein, and Billy Graham all in one.

I barely made it through my message. All the way home I thought about the way this girl saw my husband. It jolted me to look at him through another woman's eyes!

How does your husband's secretary see him? A wife should see her husband across the room and smile inside that she knows him as no one else does. Other women can look and admire, but he is hers to possess. One writer has suggested a woman should have a "holy lust" for her husband. The word lust is used carefully, meaning a strong desire to possess or enjoy. There is a difference in being possessive and possessing! The desire to know all there is of your husband to know, to own him completely, and to be totally possessed of him sexually is not being possessive." [3]

Are you in love with your husband? Oh, I know you love him. He's been around a long time, and you're used to him. Are you in love with him? How long has it been since your heart throbbed when you looked at him? We all hate to be taken for granted. Your husband needs to be told that you love him, and that he is attractive to you. Tonight, get your eyes off the dirty dishes long enough to really look at him. Then open your mouth (pry it open, if necessary) and tell him you love him and desire him.

LET YOURSELF GO!

In chapter 8, Solomon and his wife are alone in the palace. She desires to make love with her husband and aggressively takes the initiative. As part of their loveplay, and as her way of arousing her husband's sexual interest, she dances nude before him. As she dances, she coyly says to him, "Why do you gaze at the Shulammite, as at the dance of the two companies?" (The "dance of the two companies" means the dance of the Mahanaim, containing movements as magnificent and transporting as the dance of an angel, and as sensuous as the Near-Eastern dancer.) It seems rather obvious why he was gazing at her!

Solomon replies, "How beautiful are your feet in sandals, O prince's daughter! The curves of your hips are like jewels, the work of the hands of an artist" (7:1, NASB).

In case you didn't know, men are aroused by the sight of the female body. The world exploits this to the extreme. Because the world misuses the body, some women feel they should be the opposite of the world. If the world exposes the body, they will conceal it. They are not going to be like those nasty women in the *Playboy* centerfold!

I am disgusted by the blatant exploitation of sex. Recently, while searching the theatre section of the newspaper to find a good children's movie, I was sickened at the multitude of X-rated movie advertisements. They infuriate me because they degrade God's gift and cheapen it.

We glorify God in our bodies, not only by abstaining from the improper use of sex, but by the proper and holy use of our bodies in the sexual relationship. The world is wrong to expose the body, but a wife is *just* as wrong to conceal it from her husband. God's Word says husbands and wives are to enjoy and be aroused by the sight of one another's bodies. God created your husband to be aroused by *your* body!

Why don't wives provocatively display their bodies?

1. *They have too many inhibitions.* Everyone has at least a few—and they're crippling to a healthy marriage. We'll deal with this in detail in the next chapter.

2. *They don't like their bodies.* One wife told me she didn't like her husband to see her without clothing because she was sure he was looking at the roll around her middle!

There are some things about our bodies we cannot change, but there are many we can! Our weight is one of them. I wish I knew of a super diet, where all you'd have to do is pray and the pounds would fall off! I struggle constantly with my weight and know that when I am slender I feel much better about myself and feel much more attractive with my husband. If you need to lose weight, do it! If you need to exercise, do it! You can spend the rest of your life "wishing" you liked your figure. I've found dieting one of the best ways to learn more self-control. Since self-control is part of the fruit of the Spirit (Gal. 5:22–23), we should actively desire it. You'll get a double bonus—lose weight and become more spiritual at the same time!

Solomon continues to praise his wife as she dances, and he says "I will climb the palm tree, I will take hold of its fruit stalks" (7:8, NASB). To climb the palm tree was to fertilize it. Solomon was saying he intended to make love to his wife.

Then his wife says, "It goes down smoothly for my beloved, flowing gently through the lips of those who fall asleep. I am my beloved's and his desire is for me" (7:9–10, NASB). She expresses that she is totally his and available to please him. She thrills in the fact that Solomon desires her physically.

God's picture of marriage, painted in Scripture, describes a beautifully satisfying and free relationship. I pray that these few passages have shown you what God has in mind for every Christian marriage. When He tells you to enjoy sex freely and *joyfully* with your husband, He means *get after it!*

THE CREATIVE LOVER

Chapter Ten

I. BREAKING THE RESPONSE BARRIER

God's picture of marriage as a beautifully satisfying and free sexual relationship is often never realized in many marriages. Couples who do not experience this unifying physical oneness are unable to respond. For a man, this could mean impotence (the inability to have an erection) or premature ejaculation (an orgasm occurring immediately or shortly after entry). For a woman, the inability to respond usually results in the inability to have an orgasm. For some women, however, it means the inability to feel at all sexually. For others it means a total lack of interest in their sexual relationships with their husbands.

CAUSES OF A LACK OF RESPONSE

GOAL ORIENTATION

Often, when a woman has difficulty responding sexually, it is because she fears she won't have an orgasm. The goal of the sexual union becomes the female orgasm; or for a man, overcoming impotence. In contrast to this, the goal of sexual union should be the giving and receiving of love.

A wife who has been unable to achieve orgasm focuses on this failure. She begins to dread every lovemaking time because she is afraid she will fail once again.

A wife who has not achieved sexual orgasm is usually in an unfortunate situation. In her sexual experiences with her husband, she is sometimes slightly aroused, but never satisfied.

Secretly she is disappointed but does not admit it. Sexually, she had expected much in marriage, and rightly so, but she has received little. She is careful to meet her husband's sexual needs, but secretly wonders if there is something wrong with her. As the weeks pass into months, and the months pass into years, the same pattern prevails—slightly aroused, but never satisfied. Gradually she becomes nervous, and irritable. The experience becomes distasteful to her. She puts if off as long as possible.[1]

It *is* important for a woman to achieve orgasm regularly, yet this should not be the goal of the sexual union. Fear of failure is the greatest barrier to achieving success. A woman can be a skillful and exciting lover to her husband even if she never has an orgasm. If she relaxes and enjoys loving her husband and being loved by him, there is a much greater probability that she will learn to achieve orgasm.

THE SPECTATOR ROLE

One of the most damaging barriers to sexual stimulation is playing the role of "spectator" in your sexual union. Instead of getting involved, instead of forgetting everything else and letting sexual arousal happen naturally, a person may adopt this role because he or she is afraid of failing to respond. Mentally they set themselves aside and "watch" to see if they will respond. Because they are not involved, they cannot respond, thus beginning a vicious cycle of hoping, "watching," and failing.

IT'S ALL HIS FAULT!

Some women blame their husbands for their own lack of response. Perhaps it's his sexual approach. "Do you wanna do it?" Or perhaps they feel if their husbands knew more about sex or were more tender, or less gross, or more anything, *then* they would be able to respond.

Certainly husbands need to learn and grow in the area of sex just as wives do! Personally, however, I'm convinced that most women have the *ability* to respond, if they want to. Much of a woman's response (or lack of it) is centered in her will and her mind. Some of us need to look at our own weaknesses instead of majoring on our husbands'.

THOSE AWFUL MYTHS

Prevalent myths today involving sex include the sex-is-dirty myth, the size-of-sexual-organs-affects-performance myth, and the men-enjoy-sex-but-women-don't myth. If either partner accepts these myths as true, it can seriously affect his or her sexual response.

Other barriers to response can include bad experiences in childhood, dissatisfaction with marriage partner, lack of male leadership in the home, or male orgasmic dysfunction. If in the eyes of the wife the husband is a social bore, financial failure, or "the second best man," negative signals can be generated, and the woman does not respond. Pinpointing the trouble spot, one doctor said, "A major hindrance to sexual adjustment in marriage is the lack of time for sexual experience. Many couples hurry hurry through life and through their sexual experiences, for a lack of time."

LOOKING TOWARD RESPONSE

GET THE FACTS

I have been amazed at how uninformed many people are about sexual matters! Often a man and woman marry, each thinking the other knows all they need to know about a sexual relationship, when in reality they both lack even the most basic knowledge! I have talked to bright, intelligent young women who did not know (for the first several years of marriage) that a woman could or should experience an orgasm! We need to learn all we can. I feel a married couple should read at least one new book a year about their physical relationship. The list of books at the end of this chapter will help you get started!

SURRENDER TO YOUR ROLE

Examine yourself first. What is your attitude toward manhood and womanhood? Do you resent the man's role and wish it were yours or are you excited about your role as a woman and about being a *creative counterpart* to your husband?

I wish you could meet Janice. My friendship with her began as I was preparing to give my first Creative Counterpart Seminar. As a sharp, competitive businesswoman with a colossal salary, Janice is capable, deadly efficient, and strong. Janice approached me coolly and said, "I'm coming to your seminar Wednesday, and it had better be good. This will be the first time I've taken off from work in twelve years. You had better be studying." Her whole manner said, in essence, "Just try to teach *me* something. I dare you!"

Arriving at the seminar before the doors were open, Janice was ready for the attack. I could sense her challenging spirit and tried not to look at her as I spoke! After the concluding message, she waited to speak with me. She said, "I'm going to give you the greatest compliment I have ever given a woman. I wish I could trade brains with you. For thirty-three years I have believed exactly the opposite of everything you said today, and I see how terribly wrong I have been. I am determined to change. So watch out, Linda Dillow, because in one week I will be more submissive than you are!" The change hit her household like a bombshell.

Her husband, who had always followed her, began to take the lead. Her children, who had disliked her as a person, grew to adore her. And Janice herself, always a unique person, was now becoming a godly one. She had told me after the seminar that she was starting at minus ten—and she was! Soon, however, the minus changed to a plus, and the change was so great that friends visiting in her home said she was a totally different person!

Janice told me later that she had always resented being a woman. She was as smart as most men and smarter than many! Janice changed as she surrendered to the role for which God had created her. She even surprised herself because she loved it! The changes permeated into every area of her life and marriage, even into her sexual relationship with her husband.

We became close friends, and one evening as we were chatting she said, "Linda, there is one aspect of my marriage I have never shared with you. Despite my leading and running the family, we had a good marriage, except in the area of our sexual relationship. During our entire thirteen years of marriage, I was unable to have an orgasm and this greatly disturbed my husband. Since we are wealthy and could do so, we traveled to twenty states seeking help. We saw gynecologists, psychiatrists, and sex doctors. I had my head shrunk, my body shrunk, even had an operation, and yet nothing changed.

"One week after attending your seminar and yielding to all God wanted me to be, I experienced an orgasm. My husband was so excited he paced the floor most of the night saying, 'I don't believe it!' "

Some of you may carry resentments like Janice did. Ask God right now for the proper attitude. Begin to focus on all God wants you to be as a woman. Surrender to your role as a *creative helpmate* to your husband, to all we have discussed in this book about the role of the wife.

View your husband with new eyes! Ask God to let you see him anew, afresh. If you have not experienced an orgasm, or do so rarely, release this as the ultimate goal of your sexual union. Instead, love your husband and enjoy learning what pleases you sexually. God will take care of the results!

OPEN LINE TO YOUR HUSBAND

God wants you and your husband to communicate openly and freely in every area of your relationship, including sex. Perhaps you could try reading the Song of Solomon together from The Living Bible, reading one of the books I will suggest, or listening to the tapes on the sexual relationship. I cannot stress enough the importance of communication in this area. Probably 50 percent of all sexual problems can be solved by open, honest, and loving communication.

WE SHALL OVERCOME

In a survey taken of 500 Christian men and women, 40% of the women said the biggest problem in their physical relationship is that they are too inhibited. As I talk and counsel with women, I discover this same problem again and again. Inhibitions can be crippling! We must overcome them! I have had the privilege of sharing the following steps toward overcoming inhibitions with hundreds of women who have profited from them. I pray they will be helpful to you, too!

1. *Renew your mind.* Our ideas about sex often differ from what God had in mind. He wants us to realize and put into practice in our own lives the glorious picture He paints of marriage in the Song of Solomon. Reread it, and ask God to give you *His* attitude. Saturate your mind with all available information one the beautiful, free, sexual relationship God has given a husband and wife.

2. *Memorize and meditate on God's viewpoint.* God says that His word is like a two-edged sword, piercing into our lives. For years, you have had at least some negative thoughts and feelings about sex, and God wants to change all that through His Word!

A woman came to me for counseling and expressed concern about the inhibitions that kept her from being the creative lover she wanted to be and that her husband *definitely* wanted her to be! We talked about many things during our time together, but at the top of the list I suggested memorizing passages from Scripture such as 1 Corinthians 7, Proverb 5, and the Song of Solomon. Knowing what a fantastic effect God's Word has on the situation it addresses (and fearing she might not do the memory work), I told her

I would call her the following Tuesday so she could repeat her verses to me. I proceeded to write in my Priority Planner for that day, "Call Marilyn." She knew me well enough to know I do everything written in my planner like a robot!

I called Marilyn the following Tuesday, and the first thing she said was, "Do you have a cup of coffee?" Coffee in hand, I sat down to listen as she repeated ten to fifteen verses from memory! When I asked if it had helped, she replied she could hardly believe the difference.

"Throughout the day, I memorized and meditated on the Scriptures and found that I had an excited anticipation about our sexual relationship," she said. "During lovemaking, when negative thoughts would come, I would think about the passages I had learned and found that the tension would leave. At this rate, I just might memorize the whole Song of Solomon!"

3. *Decide with your will to be God's version of a creative lover.* So much of change starts with a decision. All change is hard and much of it takes time, but you can't begin until you decide, "Yes, God. I want to do it Your way." Jane had a crummy marriage and an even crummier view of sex. It was animalistic, in her opinion, and she wanted little to do with it. Her husband was not a Christian, and thus she considered sex with him as only physical, and rejected him. She came to me wanting me to agree with her view; needless to say I didn't. As we talked together, I shared God's view of the sexual relationship and encouraged her to decide to be God's version of a creative lover. Because she lived in another state, I doubted if I would ever know the outcome.

One year later I was speaking in her city, and she walked into the room. Her appearance was so changed that I hardly recognized her. There was a softness about her, a new quality of happiness and peace. Coming up to me she said, "Linda, you won't believe what happened." I said I'd believe anything because I could see it in her face. Out poured a story of two people married over twenty-five years who had learned anew to love one another, to touch one another and to care.

She talked on and told me of her first attempt at a weekend away. "I took him out to dinner and had reservations at the motel across the street. All he talked about during dinner was the movie on TV that night. I was sure my plans were to end in disaster and we would watch the tube all night. Not exactly what I had planned. And Linda, would you believe that just as we left the restaurant the electricity for the entire block went out and stayed out until after the ten o'clock news! We went to our motel room by candle-light and had no lights or TV set all evening!" She went on to tell me that her nineteen-year-old daughter had told her she had never seen a marriage she would want, especially her mother and father's. Jane told me, "Linda, by God's grace it will be our marriage she will want." God is so gracious. He even turned off electricity when needed!

4. *Do your part—your 100 percent.* In the early years of our marriage, Jody asked me to tell him in detail everything I wanted him to do to please me sexually, and then to tell him everything I was going to do to please *him.* I said (gulp!), "In detail?" I was totally embarrassed. I could barely think these things, much less verbalize them! I knew, however, that I could claim embarrassment and refuse to tell him or swallow my embarrassment and tell him freely how I was going to love him. It was embarrassing the first time, but later the embarrassment grew less and finally faded completely.

I have met many women who claim "embarrassment." They feel that in a year or two they will be more ready to respond as their husbands would like. That may be true for some, but it seems to me that the longer they wait, the harder it will be to overcome their embarrassment. After making the decision in your will to go God's way, *you* must do all you can to change. God will do the rest.

5. *Give God time to work.* I have known women who, after

implementing these principles, were released of their inhibitions overnight. For others it has been a gradual process. God works individually with each of us. If you have incorporated these principles into your own relationship, you're halfway there! Now give God the Holy Spirit time to work on the inside. He specializes in changed hearts!

II. BREAKING THE CREATIVITY BARRIER

BE TOTALLY AVAILABLE

We read in 1 Corinthians 7 that we no longer have authority over our own bodies in marriage, but our husbands do. One doctor recited this verse to a female patient who was having sexual problems in her marriage. Looking at him in abject horror, she told him if she were totally available to her husband, they would never get out of bed! The wise doctor reassured the distraught patient they wouldn't have intercourse nearly as often as she feared. "Someone who bangs on the door forty times when it stays locked," he said, "only knocks once if you open right away."

Many wives who haven't reached sexual harmony with their husbands find them making some kind of advance nearly every night. These women are afraid they will be asked to participate more often then they can bear if they let down the barriers. Actually, a man who has intercourse as often as he wants finds that in a week or two the pressure of his physical urge is relieved, and the psychological pressure to overcome resistance no longer applies. So his sex pace tapers off.

One man told my husband his wife was available to him in spurts. "After she attends Linda's seminar or reads a book on sex or after we have a knock-down, drag-out fight about sex, she is more available and has a good attitude." He said, "I know from experience it will only last a few days. So when she is responsive, I take advantage of it. Then because I do, my wife thinks all I ever think about is sex!"

Have you ever been on a diet? (I can hear you moaning.) When you're on a diet, all you can think about is food. When you can eat all you want, however, you're not nearly so interested in food. It's the same with sex. When a man or woman knows they will be rejected, they very likely become consumed with what they can't have. When a man knows his wife is totally available, his desire will gradually level off. It may take some time, but as he sees that you are eager to love and be loved by him, the driving, insistent nature of your lovemaking will be replaced by a more relaxed, secure, and loving type.

NEVER AGAIN

A woman called me recently and said, "I have a problem. My husband wants to make love very often! Sometimes its several times a day and often at two and again at four in the morning! We've had horrible fights. I've screamed at him and told him he was oversexed. Today he walked out of the house and told me to forget the whole thing. He said, 'I'll never approach you again.' Now, I'm really scared. I have heard you publicly state that your goal in life is to be a godly woman. Well, let me tell you, my goal in life is to make that man scream for mercy!" (I told her I would pray for her!) Later, she called to say she felt she was succeeding when she approached her husband sexually while he was watching TV and he said, "Please, let me finish this program first!"

She discovered she had to prove to him she was totally available by being aggressive toward him. It seems to be especially helpful for a woman to be aggressive when she is trying to convince her husband that her attitude has changed.

She discovered that for the first time her husband was truly satisfied. Contrary to the popular opinion of many women, sex is not just physical to a man! When this woman was warm, responsive, and aggressive toward her husband, he felt he was *loved* and not just *endured*. His psychological needs of acceptance and love were met, and his frantic desire for sexual relations abated. He was still very active sexually, but their relationship was much improved because of her new attitude.

TOTAL AVAILABILITY IS CHOOSING TO GIVE

A man told my husband that even when his wife satisfied him physically, he came away with a need. He said, "I feel she hasn't really given or enjoyed, but just put up with me. I need another sexual release again quickly, because I guess I'm longing for that total oneness and release that comes when both partners completely give of themselves. I know that if I was satisfied physically, emotionally, and spiritually I wouldn't walk around thinking about sex, wanting it and aching inside."

Picture this: You are busily making Christmas presents. The children are finally in bed, and for the first time that day you have a chance to do something you want and need to do. You are totally engrossed in your work as your husband walks in with that special gleam in his eye.

At this point you have a choice. You can say, "Oh, Honey, not tonight," or you can decide and choose to love this man God has given you. Your initial response may be, "Oh, no." You can change that immediately to "Oh, yes!" by an act of will. Once you are in his arms, you have more choices to make. If he is kissing you madly and you are still thinking about the Christmas gifts, it just won't work. Decide to think about loving him and ask God to fill you with genuine desire. I'm convinced that much of a woman's sexual response is in her brain! Dwell on how nice his body feels and what a privilege it is to love him, and your thoughts of the Christmas presents will fade away!

BE AGGRESSIVE!

I'm convinced most men long for their wives to be more aggressive! A man wants to know you long for him just as he longs for you. In a survey of 500 men and women, 40 percent of the men said the biggest problem in their sexual relationship was that their wives were not aggressive enough. As I mentioned before, 40 percent of the *wives* complained of their inhibitions, which is the same problem stated another way.

Some contemporary books have made suggestions for being aggressive which would cause some of you to rise up in alarm and shriek, "But that is not me." That is precisely the reason I won't suggest how *you* should be aggressive with your own husband. Each of us is an individual, and we each have a different husband. So no pet formula will work for all of us. God wants to work in innovative, exciting ways in each of our lives. Ask God to show you some clever things you can do to make your marriage a love affair. Be willing however, to put aside the inhibitions!

One woman who is old enough to be my mother, said, "I asked God to show me 'my thing,' and after thirty years of marriage it was about time! I decided one evening, after taking a shower, to ask my husband to put cream on my back (it was winter, and you know how your skin gets dry). Then I got really brave and asked him to put cream all over my body! Well, that led to other things, and later I told him about hearing your seminar and reading your book and deciding to try something new!" Her husband's enthusiatic response was, "Honey, I hope that was chapter one because I can't wait for two, three, and four!"

Now if your husband is not used to this sort of thing, tread lightly! One woman, on Halloween night, put a mink coat over her nude body and rang the front doorbell, knowing her husband would answer the door. When he opened the door, she opened the mink coat and said, "Trick or Treat!" Her poor husband was so shocked that he fell backwards and hit his head on the coffee table, resulting in a concussion!

Men are physically designed to respond to sight. Keep this in mind when considering aggressive tactics. Too often, wives approach their husbands the way *they* like to be approached (candles, romance, and all the trimmings) and husbands approach their wives the way they, the husbands, like to be approached—more physically and directly. Get to know your own husband and his preferences. If what he wants is the Dance of the Mahanaim, then put on your dancing sandals!

I received a very special letter from the husband of a woman who attended my seminar. He and his wife were both in their fifties and had a good marriage relationship. He said, "Please keep telling women how important it is to be more aggressive with their husbands in the area of sex. My wife has always been sweet, submissive, and loving, but there has never been anything like what we have now!"

One woman wrote me a note, asking, "How far should I let my husband go?" (Does this remind you of high school?) My answer to her was this: I believe, from Scripture, that anyway or anywhere you want to touch, kiss, fondle, and love your husband's body, or be loved yourself, is right and good in God's eyes. The limits are what is pleasurable to both of you.

BE CREATIVE!

You can become a Rembrandt in your sexual art, or you can stay at the paint-by-number stage.[2] What have you done creatively this week to make your sexual relationship exciting? In fact, what have you done creatively in your sexual relationship in the past year (or should I say ten years)?

LUNCHEON SPECIAL

One woman complained that her children stayed up so late that she and her husband had very little time together. I asked her if she had ever invited him home for a special luncheon. I suggested she send him an invitation listing the luncheon menu, making it clear that there would be a very special dessert, and if he liked he could have dessert first!

She called a few weeks later to say she hadn't had the courage to write the invitation yet, but had called and invited him for lunch and couldn't believe how fast he made it home!

CANDLELIGHT DINNER FOR TWO

If you have no children or small children who go to bed early, you can plan candlelight dinners after eight. You don't have to make an elaborate dinner—it can be the same spaghetti you served the children at six.

I remember well one candlelight dinner we had. I thought the children were asleep, but no such luck! Peering around the corner were two angels in white nightgowns saying, "What are you doing? Oh, what fun, can we have candles, too?" So, next morning we all had a candlelight breakfast!

One creative woman whose husband was an airline pilot and had a strange schedule, told me she fixed "candlelight breakfasts" at 5:00 A.M. before her husband left for a flight. She said it is very quiet and they have a wonderful time talking, eating, and loving each other. Of course some wives might not *want* to get up at 5:00 A.M.

CREATIVE FOOTBALL

As football season approaches, most American wives shudder. This is especially true in Dallas, where we see so much football mania! One Christian friend was dreading the onslaught of the season. Before the regular games began, her husband was watching the preseason games. On one particular night, the game began very late. She *knew* she should go in and show an interest, but really wanted to go to bed with a book. Instead, she forced herself into the TV room.

After watching a few minutes of the game, she decided to make the evening fun! She suggested to her husband that while the Cowboys were playing on the screen, they'd watch. But as soon as the football play was over, *they* would start playing! They watched for a few minutes and when the play was over, he would say, "Rub my back until the next play." The next time, it was her turn, and she might say, "Kiss me until the next play!"

This went on throughout the entire game, and she said, "I didn't know football could be so much fun!" After three hours of this, they were super-ready to make love. Even football can be exciting—it depends on how creative you are!

SWEDISH MASSAGE

There is nothing as relaxing as an all-body massage! It helps you relax, gives a feeling of contentment, and is perfect as a prelude to lovemaking. Hand lotion or heated safflower oil is perfect applied with a hand vibrator. What a wonderful way to spend an evening: talking, laughing, and gently loving one another's bodies.

I LOVE AN AMBUSH

I must repeat once more the importance of weekends alone! Be creative and surprise your husband with one! Many motels have "weekend specials" which include the room and food in a package deal. But remember the two key words— plan and persevere!

One rainy Friday night Jody and I were speaking together. I had planned a surprise retreat for the two of us and spent the afternoon packing the suitcase, preparing the food, and driving across town to get the key to our hideaway cabin.

As I was leaving the house, the children cried, "Mommy, we don't want you to go." I faltered but continued on. (Their crying stopped two seconds after I had gone, of course.) Everything went wrong and, close to tears, I wondered if it was worth it!

After we finished speaking that evening we walked to the car, and Jody said, "What's the suitcase for?"

I said, "I'm whisking you away to Holly Lake Ranch for the weekend."

He said, "Honey, thank you. I need that so much!" I forgot the hassle of the afternoon immediately!

It is such fun to sleep until noon, eat dinner at 10:00 P.M., and do whatever you want. It's a breath of fresh air to a marriage!

Picking up the phone I heard my dear friend Sara say, "It's not worth it; I really don't even want to go." Momentarily Sara was to deposit one of her children with me and escape alone with her husband for the weekend. I reassured her that I often experienced the same feelings. Often when making arrangements for the children, dog, cat, mail, etc., *you* feel like staying home!

Two days later Sara picked up her daughter and said, "I never really believed you that it was such fun to go to a motel with your husband. We have a great relationship and good communication, but what a joy to be free just to concentrate on him alone with no schedules or interruptions. It was *wonderful,* and we both can't wait to go again!"

SIX HOURS AWAY

Maybe you would love to be alone with your husband, but cannot arrange an entire weekend right now. Have you ever thought about a date at a motel? There are many nice motels for a reasonable price. You can take a picnic lunch or go out to dinner and come back to your room, plug in your popcorn popper (or whatever snacks you like), and talk and share and love all evening with no interruptions. You can leave the children with a baby-sitter at six and be home at midnight!

Now some of you might not like the idea of going to a motel with your husband. I'm not quite sure *why,* but I know someone will complain. Just remember, I am not suggesting you do *any* of the things I have mentioned. These are only suggestions to get the old gray matter perking. God wants to work in the context of *your* personality and *your* relationship, but as my husband aptly puts it, "If *nothing* aggressive or creative appeals, maybe their personalities need a little changing!"

There are many creative things I can suggest, but *you* must start thinking and come up with your own! Remember, special times together are important, and cannot be stressed enough, but the most important thing is *your attitude.* Does your husband *know* you are *available* and *excited* about him as your lover? God gave him to you as your "beloved and your friend." Let him in on the secret!

Suggested Reading List

Belliveau, Fred and Richter, Lin. *Understanding Human Sexual Inadequacy.* New York: Bantam Books. $1.25.

Bird, Joseph and Lois. *The Freedom of Sexual Love.* New York: Doubleday, 1970. $1.75.

Deutsch, Roland M. *The Key to Feminine Response in Marriage.* New York: Random House, 1968. $7.95.

Dillow, Joseph. *Solomon on Sex.* Nashville: Thomas Nelson, 1977. $6.95.

LaHaye, Tim and Beverly. *The Act of Marriage.* Grand Rapids, Mich.: Zondervan, 1976. $3.95.

Miles, Herbert J. *Sexual Happiness in Marriage.* Grand Rapids, Mich.: Zondervan, 1967. $1.75.

Rice, Shirley. *Physical Unity in Marriage.* Norfolk, Va.: Tabernacle Church, 1973. $1.75. Available by writing Tabernacle Church, 7120 Granby Street, Norfolk, Va. 23505.

Wheat, Ed. *Sexual Problems and Sexual Techniques* (tapes). Bible Believers Cassettes. 130 N. Spring Street, Springdale, Arkansas. 72764. $18.00 for set of two tapes.

THE CONSISTENT RESPONDER

Chapter Eleven

"The ways of a woman fathom none, from mood to mood she goes, and when a man's expecting one, another one she shows!" [1]

Too many of us are controlled by our emotions—by the way other people respond to us, by our circumstances, and by the way we feel about ourselves at the moment. God wants us to learn to be a consistent responder right now, where we live, not next year when things are better!

Each of you is at a different point in your life, each of you has a different husband and different needs in your life. Some of you are very excited about all you have read and are already trusting God to do His 100 percent, while you are striving to do your 100 percent. Others of you perhaps wonder if it is possible for your marriage to *ever* be what it should, and you doubt if you'll succeed as a *creative counterpart*.

Follow me mentally back through the book, past sex, submission, reverence, and priorities, to God's game plan. We talked about all He had done for us in the past and is now doing on a daily basis. With God, *all* things are possible! There is *no* temptation too great; no problem in your life or in your marriage that is too hard for God! If God is on our side, how can we fail? There are three essential ingredients in a happy marriage:[2] (1) Accept your circumstances. (2) Accept your husband. (3) Accept yourself. Our circumstances will fail, our husbands will fail, and perhaps hardest of all, we will fail, but God will *never* fail.

THOSE UNPREDICTABLE CIRCUMSTANCES

After Jody graduated from seminary, we headed for the snow country of upstate New York to work with college students at Cornell University.

Friends had rented us an old home in the country, and in we moved, with one toddler and another coming soon. The next day I turned on the water and nothing happened! Racing across the street to the landlords, I quickly told them the problem and requested they have it turned on again. It was then I learned there was no way to turn on the water because the house was built on a well! Being a city girl, I didn't know much about wells, but it soon became clear that when a well has no water, it has no water!

The Dillows were without water for six weeks. I gained a healthy appreciation for that precious commodity! The landlord was finally forced to drill another well. Because of our faith in Christ, he asked us to pray about it and tell him where to drill. As I gulped, Jody said, "Honey, if God can provide water for two million thirsty Jews in the desert, He can provide water for the Dillows on Snyder Hill Road."

Jody suggested a drilling site and one of the best wells in the area was found! As a result of this, God worked in the lives of our landlords, increasing their faith, and using the whole situation to give us a new relationship with them!

During the six weeks without water, we made a daily pilgrimage to a Christian neighbor's home to take baths and do diapers. During our "daily bath time," the woman and I began to talk about having an evangelistic coffee in her home. It was the beginning of an exciting ministry in this town.

God used our "no water" situation in many ways. I would meet people at the grocery store who would say, "Oh, I know who you are, those people without water." We became well-known in the community and were able to share the love of God with many because of our "unfortunate circumstance."

"God causes all things to work together for good to those who love God, to those who are called according to His purpose" (Rom. 8:28, NASB). All things are not good, but

God promises good will result for those who love Him and are called according to His purpose!

There are difficult circumstances in the life of every person, in every marriage. We each have a choice; when the hard times come we can put up our fists and fight with anger and resentment, or we can give the situation to God and trust He will cause good to come out of even a bad situation. The first choice breeds discontent and frustration. The second breeds the fruit of the Spirit—love, joy, peace, patience, kindness, goodness, gentleness, and self-control.

God promises to produce godly qualities in our lives as we properly respond to trials. "We also rejoice in our sufferings, because we know that suffering produces perseverance; perseverance, character; and character, hope. And hope does not disappoint us, because God has poured out his love into our hearts by the Holy Spirit, whom he has given us" (Rom. 5:3–5, NIV). Do any of you need perseverance in your life? Or character? Or hope? I do! God has asked us to respond to trials by thanking Him!

By thanking God for the unreliable and difficult circumstances we are saying, "God, you are the blessed controller of all things. You are sovereign and in control. I don't understand all that is happening, but I thank you and trust you to teach me what you want me to learn, and to work it all together for good." God commands us to thank Him and is pleased when we do. "In everything give thanks; for this is the will of God for you in Christ Jesus" (1 Thess: 5:18, NASB).

Giving thanks is different from "being thankful." I am thankful for my husband and three children and feel overwhelmed sometimes with gratitude for them. When I give thanks to God for a trial or difficult circumstance, it is not a *feeling* of thankfulness but a *decision* of my will to choose to trust God and thank Him in spite of my feelings!

PAUL—THE CONSISTENT RESPONDER
When Paul wrote the book of Philippians, he was in jail.

How difficult it must have been for him! God had given him the responsibility of taking the gospel to all the known world, and here he sat, day after day, in a jail. What could possibly come out of this situation?

> And I want you to know this, dear brothers: Everything that has happened to me here has been a great boost in getting out the Good News concerning Christ. For everyone around here, including all the soldiers over at the barracks, knows that I am in chains simply because I am a Christian. And because of my imprisonment many of the Christians here seem to have lost their fear of chains. Somehow my patience has encouraged them and they have become more and more bold in telling others about Christ. (Phil 1:12–14, TLB).

Paul had been terribly beaten, was in jail for an undetermined length of time, and yet as he wrote to the Philippians, the theme of "joy" is evident. Paul did not live *in* his circumstances or *under* his circumstances but *above* them!

> I have learned to be content whatever the circumstances. I know what it is to be in need, and I know what it is to have plenty. I have learned the secret of being content in any and every situation. . . . I can do everything through him who gives me strength (Phil. 4:11–13, NIV).

God never said your personal or marriage problems were easy, but He said He will give you the strength, so why not thank Him for it in advance! Thank God for your circumstances right now. Give your burdens to Him, and He'll give you His peace in exchange.

As you begin to put what you have learned about being a *creative counterpart* to work, your circumstances will fail. Maybe the first time you plan a candlelight dinner, the baby will get sick and you will hold a baby in your arms all night instead of being in your husband's arms as planned! Or perhaps you *finally* are going on a date with your husband, and the car breaks down, or he is unexpectedly called out on business, or one or both of you get the flu. You have a choice, you can *react* wrongly and *fight* the circumstances, or you can respond correctly and trust God to work it together for good. I can almost guarantee you that your circumstances will fail, but praise God, He *never* does!

THOSE UNPREDICTABLE HUSBANDS

Creative Carol is all ready to begin admiring her husband. As Ken comes in from work she says, "Honey, I really thank you for your hard work to provide so well for us." Proud of herself for admiring him, she awaits his response. Whammo! Ken replies, "I know you don't mean that; you're always complaining about the long hours I work." Ken's response was not exactly what she had been hoping for.

Carol now has two choices. She can bite back with, "Just see if I ever compliment you again!" Or she can ignore the hurt and say, "Honey, you're right, I have been wrong to complain. I really am thankful and proud of you."

Perhaps one creative wife will try the Dance of the Mahanaim for her husband and he'll laugh (that would be a hard one)! Our natural response when we're hurt is to take a step forward and hit back. ("You clod, I knew it would never work. I felt dumb doing that silly dance anyway!") The supernatural response is to step back and respond with a blessing.

"Do not repay evil with evil or insult with insult, but with blessing, because to this you were called so that you may inherit a blessing" (1 Pet. 3:9, NIV). Your husbands are very human and may not always give just the response you were hoping for. God asks you to be faithful and do your 100 percent—not because of what you are going to get in return, but because you want to be a faithful servant. At the same time, though, God also said that when you return a blessing for an insult, you will inherit a blessing!

How do we give a blessing? By looking to God rather than to our husbands or our circumstances.

Elisabeth Elliot was a woman who returned a blessing for a great evil. Her husband, Jim, was one of five men who sought to bring the gospel of Christ to the Auca Indians, a very primitive tribe in South America during the 1950s. While attempting to tell the Indians of the love of Christ, all five men were killed by the Indians they tried to help.

The natural response in such a tragic situation would be to hate, to be resentful, to seek revenge. Elisabeth Elliot did exactly the opposite. Taking her small daughter with her, she went back into the Auca tribe that killed her husband. She loved them and won them to a faith in Christ. In one book about her, there is a picture of her and her daughter standing by the river while the very men who killed her husband were being baptized. Elisabeth Elliot demonstrated a supernatural response; she gave a blessing instead of responding with evil or insult.

You probably will not be asked to do what Elisabeth Elliot had to do. But you may have to return a blessing when your husband disappoints or hurts you. Instead of stepping forward and hitting back, decide to step back and respond with a blessing. I can almost promise you that your husband will fail in some way, but be assured that God will never fail you!

THAT UNPREDICTABLE ME

As you seek to be a *creative counterpart*, your circumstances may fail, your husband may fail, and, hardest of all, you will fail. We fail because we will never be perfect until we are with God.

I BLEW IT, LORD

I remember well one sunny afternoon at Southern Methodist University. I had spent three hours in a row going from sorority to sorority sharing with the girls about the excellent wife in Proverb 31. I walked home so excited about being God's woman, anxious to see Jody and put what I had talked about for three hours into practice!

Walking through the door I stopped cold. Strewn through the house, in living color, were Jody's clothes. Beginning in the kitchen were the shoes and socks, in the living room his shirt, and the rest trailing into the bedroom. Obviously he had been in a hurry to go jogging! One look at those strewn clothes, and the excellent wife was "out the window," replaced by me, "the angry wife." I blew up, screaming at Jody. Realizing what a hypocrite I was, I fell on the bed, sobbing. I had talked for three hours about the excellent wife, but I couldn't live it for three minutes! It was *hopeless!*

As I lay there sobbing, God reminded me it *wasn't* hopeless. When we're faithless, He remains faithful! Yes, I had blown it, but God loved me and forgave me, and He wanted me to forgive myself.

I'm convinced one of the greatest hindrances to growth in the Christian life is our refusal to forgive ourselves. We accept the fact that when we confess our sins He is faithful and just to forgive us our sin and cleanse us from all unrighteousness, but that's as far as it goes! In a sense, I think we feel we'll show God we're *really* sorry by moping and hating ourselves for a while.

God says He takes our sin and casts it into the deepest sea (Mic. 7:18), and then He puts up a "No Fishing" sign! He wants us to admit when we fail, then move on!

God has given me the privilege of instructing other women how to be creative wives, yet I still fail in every area discussed in this book. There are weeks when my priorities seem upside down and backwards. Once again I reevaluate them before God. There are times when the me that thinks my viewpoint is so right challenges all my husband says and is totally unsubmissive. Once again, I must ask God's forgiveness. Although I have seen exciting growth in my life, that does not mean I never fail. But my failures are fewer as I grow and learn to forgive myself and trust the Holy Spirit.

A STEP AT A TIME

Becoming a *creative counterpart* is a process. If you're on the road, you're headed toward the goal, and that's exciting! A great man once said, "It's not so important what a man is, as what he's becoming; for you shall be what you are now be-com-ing!"

I wish I could tell you that once you put down this book, magic will occur, and you will in one wave of the wand be a *creative counterpart*. It sounds terrific, but *God's* way is one step at a time. We are all habit-oriented creatures, and many of us have many bad habits! It takes three weeks to feel good about a new habit and six to make it your own. God says we are to discipline ourselves for the purpose of godliness (1 Tim. 4:7). This means we are to be *oriented* toward godliness. Our whole life ought to be disciplined (structured, set up, organized, and running day to day) toward the goal of godliness. Becoming like Jesus Christ is a process, but it's an exciting one!

Look now at the project on the next page. I've asked you to list three areas discussed in this book in which you feel the *most* competent. Maybe it is admiration (you esteem and reverence your husband), or maybe you are already a creative lover, or perhaps your priorities have always been in order. Consider all areas including priorities, God's part/your part, acceptance, admiration, submission, sex, organization in the home, and consistent response. Be as specific as you like. You can choose a general category like "priorities" or pick just one of the six priorities to zero in on. Write down your three most competent areas right now.

Next, list the three areas discussed in this book in which you feel the *least* competent. Maybe it is your priorities, or perhaps it's partner acceptance. (Are you a personal Holy Spirit?) Write down your three least competent areas right now. Take number one and write it on the calendar for this month and next month. Then take number two and put it on the calendar for the following month. As you review this book, fill out your entire calendar something like this:

Areas Feel Most Competent   *Areas Feel Least Competent*
1. Priorities   1. Submission

2. Admiration
3. Children
January—Submission
February—Sex
March—Acceptance

2. Sex
3. Acceptance

See what you're doing? Step by step over the next year, as you do your part trusting God to do His part, you will change in twelve major areas of your life! This is not the wave of the wand but transformation of your habit patterns, some that you've had for a lifetime. If you diligently follow your chart, working on one area at a time, consider the state of the union at your house in six months—in one year!

List the three areas discussed where you feel the most competent.

1.

2.

3.

January-

February-

March-

April-

May-

June-

List the three areas discussed where you feel the least competent.

1.

2.

3.

July -

August -

September -

October -

November -

December -

I have used this method for the last few years, and it has been a tremendous encouragement to me! It's so easy to read a book like this and come away ready to try all! Then, after being overwhelmed with *all,* we end up changing none! I have seen real progress in my life as step by step I have taken one area of my life and worked on it for a month, then moved on to a new area. It is exciting and rewarding to be on the path headed toward the goal!

I pray you will be precious to Him who will *always* be faithful to do His part as you diligently do yours.

Who can find an excellent wife, a Creative Counterpart? For her worth is far above rubies.

FOOTNOTES

Chapter 2

1. Eugenia Price, *Woman to Woman* (Grand Rapids: Zondervan, 1959), p. 7.
2. Derek Kidner, *The Proverbs* (Downers Grove: InterVarsity, 1972), p. 184.
3. Matthew Henry, *Matthew Henry's Commentary on the Whole Bible*, 2 vols. (Wilmington, Delaware: Sovereign Grace Publishers, 1972), II, p. 578.
4. William Mckane, *Proverbs* (Philadelphia: Westminister Press, 1970), p. 666.
5. C. H. Toy, *Proverbs*, in ICC (Edinburgh: T & T Clark, 1899), p. 545.
6. A. R. Fausset, Robert Jamieson, and David Brown, *A Commentary on the Old and New Testaments*, 6 vols. (Grand Rapids: Eerdmans, 1967), III, p. 513.

Chapter 4

1. Shirley Rice, *The Christian Home, A Woman's View* (Norfolk; Norfolk Christian Schools, 1972), p. 68.
2. Sally Meredith of Christian Family Life (Little Rock, Ark.) has contributed several helpful suggestions. The *Priority Planner* is also available from Thomas Nelson, Inc.
3. Daryl V. Hoole, *The Art of Homemaking* (Salt Lake City: Deseret Book Co., 1969), p. 90–91.

Chapter 5

1. Judith Viorst, "What Is This Thing Called Love?" *Redbook Magazine* (February, 1975).
2. *Family Life Today*, Regal Press (May, 1976).
3. Many of these categories were first listed by Helen B. Andelin, *Fascinating Womanhood* (Santa Barbara: Pacific Press, 1965), p. 36–37.

Chapter 6

1. Excerpt from *Hide or Seek* by Dr. James Dobson is Copyright © 1974 by Fleming H. Revell Company. Used by permission.

Chapter 7

1. The sequences outlined here in "Plan A," were first suggested to me by Don Meredith of Christian Family Life, Little Rock, Arkansas.

2. Larry Christenson, *The Christian Family* (Minneapolis: Bethany Fellowship, 1970), p. 42.
3. *Collegiate Challenge Magazine* (Arrowhead Springs: Campus Crusade for Christ).
4. Adapted from the Christian Family Life *Basic I Seminar Manual,* Little Rock, Arkansas.
5. W. E. Vine, *An Expository Dictionary of New Testament Words* (Westwood: Revell, 1966).
6. Vine, "gentle."
7. Vine, "quiet."
8. Alan Redpath, *Victorious Christian Living* (Old Tappan, N.J.: Fleming H. Revell, 1951), p. 166.

Chapter 8
1. Suggested by Bill Gothard, *Institute in Basic Youth Conflicts.*

Chapter 9
1. Shirley Rice, *Physical Unity in Marriage* (Norfolk: Norfolk Christian Schools, 1973), p. 19.
2. Cf. *Solomon on Sex,* by Joseph Dillow (Nashville: Thomas Nelson, Inc., 1977).
3. Shirley Rice, p. 3

Chapter 10
1. Herbert J. Miles, *Sexual Happiness in Marriage* (Grand Rapids: Zondervan, 1967), p. 124–125.
2. Marabel Morgan, *The Total Woman* (Old Tappan, N.J.: Fleming H. Revell, 1973), p. 126.

Chapter 11
1. Gladys Seashore, *The New Me* (Minneapolis: His International Services, 1972), p. 20.
2. Jill Renich, *To Have and To Hold* (Grand Rapids: Zondervan, 1972), p. 23.